MANAGING PROJECTS in MINISTRY

VINCENT WYATT HOWELL

Foreword by Stephen Butler Murray
Afterword by Vergel L. Lattimore III

JUDSON PRESS
PUBLISHERS SINCE 1824

Join our mailing list for updates and special offers.
www.judsonpress.com/mailing_list.cfm

Managing Projects in Ministry
© 2017 by Judson Press, Valley Forge, PA. All rights reserved.

Judson Press has made every effort to trace the ownership of all quotes. In the event of a question arising from the use of a quote, we regret any error made and will be pleased to make the necessary correction in future printings and editions of this book.

Unless otherwise indicated, all Scriptures quoted in this book are taken from New International Reader's Version (NIRV), Copyright © 1995, 1996, 1998, 2014 by Biblica, Inc.® Used by permission. All rights reserved worldwide.

Others Scriptures are taken from the following translations:

The Holy Bible, English Standard Version® (ESV®), copyright © 2001 by Crossway, a publishing ministry of Good News Publishers. Used by permission. All rights reserved. ESV Text Edition: 2007.

Good News Translation—Second Edition (GNT). Copyright © 1992 by American Bible Society. Used by permission.

The International Standard Version (ISV), Copyright © 1995–2014 by ISV Foundation. ALL RIGHTS RESERVED INTERNATIONALLY. Used by permission of Davidson Press, LLC.

King James Version (KJV).

The Message (MSG) by Eugene H. Peterson, copyright © 1993, 1994, 1995, 2000, 2001, 2002. Used by permission of NavPress Publishing Group. All rights reserved.

New Century Version® (NCV). Copyright © 1987, 1988, 1991 by Word Publishing, a division of Thomas Nelson, Inc. Used by permission. All rights reserved.

The Holy Bible, New International Version®. NIV®. Copyright © 1973, 1978, 1984, 2011 by Biblica, Inc.™ Used by permission of Zondervan. All rights reserved worldwide. www.zondervan.com

The New King James Version (NKJV). Copyright © 1982 by Thomas Nelson, Inc. Used by permission. All rights reserved.

Library of Congress Cataloging-in-Publication Data
Cataloging-in-Publication Data available upon request.
Contact cip@judsonpress.com.

Printed in the U.S.A.

First edition, 2017.

To my loving wife, Carolyn,
who has been my partner in life and ministry,
encouraging me throughout the years
to write and share the Good News,
and to my two wonderful children,
Naila and Vincent Jr.

Contents

Foreword

Securing church leadership strategies has become a pivotal issue for Christian congregations today, especially as the professional backgrounds of clergy have shifted. Twenty years ago, aspiring clergy went to seminary directly after college and then on to their pastoral charges, establishing a youthful clergy who brought few skills from prior professions to bear upon their ministry. Today, it is much more likely for people to attend seminary as a second, third, or even fourth career, with many seminarians now being in their forties or even fifties. Further, because fewer churches are able to hire a full-time pastor, bivocational ministry is becoming the new norm, especially for new ministers. The question of what professional skills one brings to the ministry has taken on a new importance with these shifts in the age, prior experience, and need for multivalent talents among today's clergy.

Vincent Wyatt Howell makes an important contribution to this dialogue about church leadership in arguing that project management skills are translatable to the church and ministry. While the fundamentals of project management are well-known to anyone who has business school training, Howell presents the four phases of project management through real-life ministry examples, allowing his experiences with congregational ministry to illustrate the principles of project management. For those unfamiliar with what may sound initially like corporate-world rhetoric, Howell carefully explains how inspiration and initiation, planning, execution, and evaluation and celebration are useful to clergy and lay leaders alike.

This sort of book can be written only by someone with an abundance of experience both in congregational ministry and in corporate and nonprofit organizations. In response to his call to ministry, Vincent Wyatt Howell earned his MDiv from Colgate Rochester Crozer Divinity School, was ordained in the same year, and later earned the DMin from Ecumenical Theological Seminary. Howell has served as a bivocational pastor while working as an engineering manager. Currently he serves a two-point charge in the United Methodist Church in Elmira, New York.

However, Howell also has a profound background in engineering and management. He holds a BS in industrial technology and a master's in organization and management. Howell has 36 years of international engineering management, project management, and engineering experience, including his current position as Manager of Information Security and Policy in the Display Technologies Division at Corning, Inc. Previously, he held manufacturing management and engineering positions in the defense electronics and telecommunications industry. Howell's experiences have included developing and implementing quality improvement and workforce development strategies. In 2006 Howell was awarded Corning Display Technologies' prestigious "People Development Award."

Howell's outstanding experience simultaneously in ministry and in industrial business provides a powerful background for understanding how project management skills might best be applied to an ecclesiastical audience. Howell's approach will appeal to clergy who themselves have a business background, but who have not successfully translated the skills that they developed in business to the church setting. The book provides not only a roadmap for applying project management principles to ministry, but also the biblical foundation that validates these practices within the faith tradition—an invaluable tool when working with trustees, deacons, and other church leaders.

Howell's approach will help clergy who are testing the waters, trying out different techniques, and who may not be familiar with project management principles themselves. By offering such an inviting introduction to these ideas and their practice, Howell is able to walk an unfamiliar reader into a fresh methodology for church leadership.

That said, this volume will be of tremendous use not only to clergy, but to church leadership among the laity as well. I would invite boards of trustees and deacons to read this together, welcoming the sort of dialogue that would come out of such groups examining how the church runs in light of these project management principles. This book may be the basis of an excellent retreat, focusing on how the church plans for its future and then executes those plans for the greatest fulfillment of its sacred mission.

As someone with an MBA and a PhD in theology who has served churches in six different denominations and now serves as a seminary president, I appreciate the thoughtful, perceptive ability with which Howell applies project management principles to the sacred work of the church as a whole and to individual ministries within the church. His use of ministry profiles makes this translation all the more clear and less treacherous. This allows the reader to step into the scenarios that are presented with ease and with the sense that we are not alone in facing these sorts of decisions in the work of ministry, which despite its collaborations often can feel quite isolating and lonely. By embracing project management skills, church leaders will find themselves encouraged to reimagine how they work with others, renewing and reenergizing the intersectional work of ministry in the church today.

Rev. Dr. Stephen Butler Murray
President and Professor of Systematic Theology and Preaching
Ecumenical Theological Seminary, Detroit, Michigan

Preface

Project management concepts have been used in business, industry, government, and a variety of organizations for many years. They are widely used for major undertakings such as building construction, church expansions, road construction projects, or industrial technology innovations. The value and growth of project management as a discipline has given rise to the project management profession, with a globally recognized body of knowledge. Project management as a profession is now well engrained in for-profit and not-for-profit organizations. A case in point is an organization many of us are familiar with—Habitat for Humanity. No Habitat construction project is done without the utilization of project management.

Why use project management tools in the church? I will answer this question from a practical experience perspective. During my pastoral experience, I have seen effective lay leadership of organizations within the church. Some leaders have developed strong leadership skills based on workshops and informal learning provided by the pastor or the denomination or by building on skills they have developed through lifelong learning in secular employment. Two key events stand out when I reflect on the need for project management in the church.

The first example occurred when I served as an assistant minister in a Rochester, New York, church with a history of 150 years of community ministry led successfully by both the pastors and laity. As the pastor aged, his ability to lead and do all the things he previously did during his twenty-five-year pastorate at this church became limited. Assistant ministers helped, and a very active group of lay leaders served at a high level of leadership engagement as well. Teaching ministries, youth ministries, responsibilities to the broader denomination, community programs, preaching ministries, and lay programs all continued without interruption.

As an assistant minister early in my pastoral experience, I often pondered why this was. My conclusion was that many of the officers of the church had been exposed to and learned from a variety of management experiences in corporate vocations or leadership roles they played in such arenas as school board, city council, and industry. Their knowledge helped build a strong leadership foundation.

The second example I heard about was at a smaller church. The church undertook a capital building project (which included beginning to gut the building) without having a project schedule, resource plan, or finance strategy. The project was not completed, and the property now stands unused.

These two examples show the necessity of providing project management tools for church leaders and laity alike. This book provides practical knowledge and tools to aid church leaders in presenting and steering effective programs and projects within their congregations. Although a number of books address the topic of project management from a secular perspective, this book provides the church with the fundamentals while demonstrating how to ground project management in a biblical foundation.

Acknowledgments

I never would have been able to write this book without significant people who have been mentors in ministry. Dr. Urias Beverly, dean of the doctor of ministry program at the Ecumenical Theological Seminary, Detroit, Michigan, encouraged me as a bivocational pastor seeking advanced ministry learning, and he has remained a supporter of my writing and contributions to the literature of practical ministry. Rev. Dr. Charles Edward Clark Jr., pastor of the People's Community Church, Detroit, and Rev. Dr. David Swink, former pastor of the Chilson Hills Church, Brighton, Michigan, in their inspiring and insightful ways, kept urging me to refine my thinking and call as to how God could use my leadership experience in the church. Truly their mentorship and advice have helped me to get to this point.

Also along this journey, I have benefited from the encouragement of several colleagues in ministry—Rev. Dr. Gloria J. Clark, Rev. Dr. Amy Green, Rev. Dr. Wayne McKinney, Rev. Dr. Vergel Lattimore (president of Hood Theological Seminary, Salisbury, North Carolina), and the late Rev. Roosevelt Simons.

I am ever grateful to the members of the Westside United Methodist Church, Elmira, New York, and of the Webb Mills United Methodist Church, Pine City, New York, whom I have pastored for the past five years. They have supported me as I write, and they have followed my leadership as we seek to make disciples for Jesus Christ for the transformation of the world.

In my early years of developing this concept, members of the Frederick Douglass Memorial A.M.E. Zion Church and the Monumental Baptist Church, both of Elmira, NY, sat in on my initial workshops. I am grateful for their participation and feedback.

I thank Rev. Rebecca Irwin-Diehl and Lisa Blair at Judson Press for their editorial assistance and for believing in this project.

Last but most important, I thank Jesus Christ my Savior, who is my inspiration. May this work glorify and give praise to God for all the things I have heard and seen.

PART ONE

Why Project Management in the Church

CHAPTER 1

$\longrightarrow$

God's Creation of Project Management
THE STORY OF NOAH

In the book of Genesis, we find the story of Noah, a man who found favor in the eyes of God during a period when evil was spreading, causing God great consternation. Noah was a righteous man, blameless among the people of his time (Genesis 6:9). He loved and obeyed God with his whole heart. Because of wickedness on the earth, God decided to wipe out the human race he had created. The Lord assigned Noah a project that would play a significant part in the divine master plan. That project was to build an ark. Thus God created the first project manager—Noah. Genesis 6:9-22 outlines the story of Noah's project.

Here is the story of Noah's family line.

Noah was a godly man. He was without blame among the people of his time. He walked with God. Noah had three sons. Their names were Shem, Ham and Japheth.

The earth was very sinful in God's eyes. It was full of people who did mean and harmful things. God saw how sinful the earth had become. All its people were living very sinful lives.

So God said to Noah, "I am going to put an end to everyone. They have filled the earth with their harmful acts. I am certainly going to destroy them and the earth. So make yourself an ark out of cypress wood. Make rooms in it. Cover it with tar inside and out. Here is how I want you to build it. The ark has to be 450 feet long. It has to be 75 feet wide and 45 feet high. Make a roof for it. Leave below the roof an opening all the way around that is a foot and a half high. Put a door in one side of the ark. Make lower, middle and upper decks. I am going to bring a flood on the earth. It will destroy all life under the sky. It will destroy every living creature that breathes. Everything on earth will die. But I will make my covenant with you. You will go into the ark. Your sons and your wife and your sons' wives will enter it with you. Bring a male and a female of every living thing into the ark. They will be kept alive with you. Two of every kind of bird will come to you. Two of every kind of animal will also come to you. And so will two of every kind of creature that moves along the ground. All of them will be kept alive with you. Take every kind of food that you will need. Store it away as food for you and them."

Noah did everything just as God commanded him.

I will provide greater detail about project management terms in later chapters, but for now I will say simply that a *project* is defined as a temporary undertaking, having a defined beginning and end (usually constrained by time, cost, and deliverables), undertaken to meet unique goals and objectives that bring about beneficial change. Furthermore, *project management* is the discipline of planning, organizing, securing, and managing resources to bring about the successful completion of specified project goals and objectives.

Clearly, when God assigned Noah the ark-building project, this was a one-time effort with defined start and end dates. Noah had to complete the ark by the time God was to send the flood. The start of the project was when God told him to "build an ark," and the end of the project was the date when God said, "Seven days from now I will send rain on the earth. It will rain for 40 days and 40 nights" (Genesis 7:4). And the deliverable was the completed ark that would house not only Noah and his family, but also two of all living creatures, including birds, and every kind of animal that moved along the ground, both male and female, and enough food to sustain everyone on the ark (see Genesis 6:18-21). The beneficial change as a result of the project was saving a representative portion of humankind and animals from the flood.

When we look at the story of Noah in light of the project management definition, we see that the ark was completed on time, and it was able to withstand the rain and flood. Initially, God specified how the ark was to be built, including dimensions and room design and the use of cypress wood and sealing tar on the roof and inside. In addition, the ark had to be open a foot and a half from the top, and there had to be a door in one side of the ark, with lower, middle, and upper decks.

To execute the project tasks successfully, Noah had to plan, organize, secure resources, and manage resources, including the time line for completing the ark successfully. For example, he had to locate and acquire cypress wood, not oak or pine, and he had to obtain the correct amount of supplies.

Without planning, the result would be a deliverable that was too long, too big, too short, or not fit to accommodate those expected to be housed. We know, however, that the project was managed successfully, for Genesis 8:3-4 says that the ship withstood the floods for more than 150 days. The project also met its objectives and was executed per God's master project plan, as demonstrated in the verse that says, "Noah did everything just as God commanded him" (Genesis 6:22).

A lot of time has passed since God initiated that first project to be managed by a divinely appointed "project manager" for the good of God's people and for the sake of humankind's reconciliation with the Lord. As God's church, we are busy conducting the business of the church, implementing programs that provide care and service, and doing projects that support various ministries for our communities. The question before each of us is, "By what means will we manage these projects?" Will we do things our way or will we follow the example of Noah by doing "everything just as God commanded"?

There are numerous ways to get things done in the church. But God demands more than good enough; God demands that we do our best: "Work at everything you do with all your heart. Work as if you were working for the Lord, not for human masters. Work because you know that you will finally receive as a reward what the Lord wants you to have. You are [servants] of the Lord Christ" (Colossians 3:23-24). With Noah as our example, our efforts must meet the high standards, vision, and objectives that God gives us for the project. Otherwise, our results will not withstand the storms of life.

Economic challenges place enormous strain on resources in local churches, so we must be ever mindful of being good stewards of the resources and gifts committed to our management. Utilizing all available tools for effective management and leadership is imperative. Project management tools can help church leaders do their work more efficiently—and potentially at a lower cost.

In short, even in the church, we must learn to execute the work of the church smarter, not harder, in order not only to survive in this age but also to implement effective ministries that serve God's people. Applying project management in the context of the church is one way to achieve this result.

CHAPTER 2

→

An Overview of
Project Management

Lay leaders must handle a variety of ministry tasks. Luke's account of the choosing of the seven deacons in Acts 6 provides a relevant example. As the number of Christ followers started to grow, the community raised a concern that the needs of some believers were being neglected. At the same time, the disciples were concerned that they were spending too much time away from preaching and teaching God's Word. To address this situation, the twelve apostles requested that the church members appoint seven lay leaders who could be charged with the administration and pastoral care needs of the congregants. With these lay leaders in place (Gk. *diakonos*; often referred to as *deacons* in English), the disciples could refocus on the priority given to them by the Lord.

To accomplish the broader ministry of the church, lay members must have appropriate leadership tools at their disposal. Since projects are typically a part of managing the church and involve joint pastoral and lay leadership—whether these projects are as small as presenting an annual Thanksgiving Dinner for the homeless or as large as purchasing or renovating a new parsonage—congregations can benefit from applying project management.

Although project management was once seen as applicable only in industry, it is now regarded as valuable in a variety of businesses and organizations, including churches.[1] Competent project leadership makes it possible for others to do good work and to produce results that give them a sense of personal power and ownership.[2] Letty Russell, a prominent feminist theologian and a longtime member of the Yale Divinity School faculty, further affirms the importance of leadership in church organizations: "Leadership is needed in Christian communities as in other human communities, but not necessarily leadership in a fixed hierarchical model. Churches are likely to grow toward partnership among their members when there is a dynamic of leadership among a variety of people and not just one leader."[3] Thus project management can become an important leadership strategy in the local church because it requires the involvement of a diverse group of people in the church and community.

Definitions

For clarity, we must define three critical components of project management. Knowledge of the terms *project, project management*, and *project manager* are fundamental to developing and implementing project management in the church.

Project

Understanding what a project is and is not, is an important starting position. Most practitioners define a project as a unique set of coordinated activities with definite starting and finishing points, undertaken by an organization to meet specific objectives within a defined schedule and cost and performance parameters.

In its *Guide to the Project Management Book of Knowledge*, the Project Management Institute defines a "project as a temporary endeavor undertaken to create a unique product or service. Temporary means that every project has a definite beginning and a definite end. Unique means that a product or service is different in some distinguishing way than all other products and services."[4]

To understand the term *project* from a social context, consider the following characteristics:

1. **Projects have a purpose.** Projects have clearly defined aims and set out to produce clearly defined results. Their purpose is to solve a problem, address a need, or provide a service in response to the problem or need. This involves analyzing needs beforehand. The end result aims at lasting social change.

2. **Projects are realistic.** Their aims must be achievable, and this means taking account both of requirements and of the financial and human resources available.

3. **Projects are limited in time.** They have a beginning and an end, and are implemented in a specific place and context.

4. **Projects are complex.** Projects call on various planning and implementation skills, and involve various partners and players.

5. **Projects are collective.** Projects are the product of a collective endeavor. They are conducted by teams, involve various partners, and cater to the needs of others.

6. **Projects are unique.** All projects stem from new ideas. They provide a specific response to a need (problem) in a specific context. They are innovative.

7. **Projects are an adventure.** Every project is different and groundbreaking; projects always involve some uncertainty and risk.

8. **Projects can be assessed.** Projects are planned and broken down into measurable steps or phases, each of which is evaluated as project activity progresses.

9. **Projects are made up of stages.** Projects have distinct, identifiable stages. From these definitions, a number of activities undertaken within the context of church operations can be considered projects. Examples of this are: plans for an evangelism strategy, planning a day care center ministry, and organizing a prayer breakfast.[5]

As distinguished from other forms of management or management processes, projects are unique, temporary, onetime events with distinct beginnings and endings. According to Timothy Kloppenborg, Arthur Shriberg, and Jayashree Venkatraman, management professors and project management consultants, each project follows a basic process referred to as the project life cycle.[6] The project life cycle is a logical sequence of activities carried out to accomplish a project's goals or objectives. Be it a large corporation, a social service nonprofit, or a church organization, all projects go through a series of stages during their lives, regardless of scope, size, or complexity. Project success depends on paying attention to the details of this process. Jason Westland, author of *The Project Management Life Cycle: A Complete Step-by-Step Methodology for Initiating, Planning, Executing & Closing a Project Successfully*, and founder of Method123.com, whose text specifically focuses on the topic of project life cycle, provides a definition of each phase of project management:

▶ **Initiation.** Within the initiation phase, the ministry problem or opportunity is identified, a solution and scope of work is defined, a project is formalized, and a project manager is appointed. It is at this phase where the project manager begins to recruit a project team to build and deliver the solution for the church or community (referred to as the customer in project management terms).

▶ **Planning.** The planning phase is critical and involves outlining the activities, tasks, dependencies, and time frames required to execute the project. Resource planning is done, which includes defining who does what, additional support people required, equipment or facilities needed, and any additional materials required. Cost and financial plans are documented, along with plans to measure and control the work to be done so that a quality product or service is delivered. In support of the total planning process, risks are identified, along with contingency plans; and communication and meeting plans are defined, along with a plan for defining if the project has been completed to the requirements and scope of the project that were agreed on.

▶ **Execution.** The execution phase is where most of the work on the project takes place by the project team. This is where the plans put together in the planning phase get done, where all of the tasks are accomplished. During this phase, the *project manager* (see page 14) and team members monitor and control project tasks and activities to assure that expected outcomes are achieved. Once the ministry outcome, product, service, or event is accepted and complete, the project team is ready to move to the closure phase.

▶ **Closure.** The final phase is closure. This is where the project manager, team, pastor, and congregation assess how well the project was done. They ask themselves, "What went well?," "What should we do differently when we do another project?," and "What lessons did we learn for future application or sharing with other teams in the organization?"[7]

Method123, Ltd., a global project management consultancy, depicts the project life cycle with the following graphic:

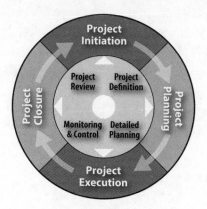

FIGURE 1
The Project Life Cycle
Used with permission by Method123, Ltd.

Project evaluation at closure is vital, for it will provide key lessons learned in project management. One of my colleagues, who spent more than thirty years in pastoral ministry and as a seminary professor, says that one of the things the church does not do well is evaluation after a project or event is completed. Providing structure in managing projects will support the evaluation step of the process.

Project Management

Understanding the definition of *project management* is paramount as we consider its application in a church setting. A church project is a unique, time-constrained event that requires planning, organizing, and resources (materials, funding, and people) to bring about the successful implementation of a ministry or church goal or objective.

Definitions of project management come from a number of sources. Fundamentally, project management is defined as "the planning, monitoring and control of all aspects of a project and the motivation of all those involved in it, in order to achieve project objectives within agreed criteria of time, cost, and performance."[8]

In their book *Project Management: A Managerial Approach*, Jack Meredith and Samuel Mantel Jr. provide a view of project management that covers the difficult problems associated with conducting a project using people and organizations that represent different cultures. They hold that "project management has emerged because of characteristics of our contemporary society that demand the development of new methods of management."[9] Of the many forces involved, two appear to have impact on the church: (1) the exponential expansion of human knowledge, and (2) the growing demand for a broad range of complex and customized services.[10]

One additional component of project management that should not be overlooked is how projects get executed. Projects generally are not a one-person effort; most are executed by a group of people, or a team.

> The project team is a critical foundation of any project, and the project leader will do well to look out for its interests even before it is assembled. Although project teams have many interests, an overriding one is simply to be able to do the project, given the time and cost constraints and the . . . services to be delivered. Other key interests are to have a smoothly running project with minimum disruption from changes and having the resources to do the job when they are needed.[11]

The project leader must understand that building an effective team requires more than simply selecting a group of people to work on the project. It involves such things as team size, ideology, interactions, and communication—along with the team development stages. Team development includes the team forming into a team or work group, getting to a point where the team members establish operating norms, including communication, working through initial and normal misunderstandings that result in building trust, and lastly, being able to work together as a cohesive group to perform the required objectives. In project management, all teams go through these stages as they establish effective team building. Both the people who lead and the people who make up the project team play pivotal roles in the team's ultimate success.

Project Manager

Every project must have a *project manager* to provide guidance and leadership to the team throughout its duration. Project management practitioner and international consultant Paul Dinsmore defines a project manager as one who is "required to wind up their projects within established schedule, budget, and quality standards."[12] To achieve project results, the project manager at times must marshal diverging or conflicting resources into harmonious unity using such skills as planning, administration, psychology, communication, optimism, salesmanship, and frugality. Regardless of whether the project is related to a technological, social, ministerial, or Christian educational program, the same skills apply.

One of the critical roles the project manager plays is that of team leader. This is especially true in the church. Unlike workers in a corporate setting, church members don't follow a leader because they are paid to do so as part of their job. They are volunteers or feel called to serve a particular ministry. So for the project manager to be effective, her followers (the project team) must have faith in her as a person who not only cares about the church but also cares about them as individuals and as a group. Otherwise, the project manager does not have a team that can effectively execute a project.

A story about a familiar team icon highlights the importance of team leader effectiveness. Lee Iacocca once asked legendary football coach Vince Lombardi what it took to make a winning team. The book *Iacocca* records Lombardi's answer (as cited by the secondary source, noteable-quotes.com):

> "There are a lot of coaches with good ball clubs who know the fundamentals and have plenty of discipline but still don't win the game. Then you come to the third ingredient: if you're going to play together as a team, you've got to care for one another. You've got to love each other. Each player has to be thinking about the next guy and saying to himself: *If I don't block that man, Paul is going to get his legs broken. I have to do my job well in order that he can do his.*[13]

"The difference between mediocrity and greatness," Lombardi said that night, "is the feeling those guys have for each other."

In the healthy church, each Christian learns to care for others. As we take seriously Jesus' command to love one another, we contribute to a winning team.

The project manager works with the pastor (who is often the sponsor of projects in the church), the congregation, and the leader board to secure the appropriate members to participate on the project team. Team members may be cross-functional, and the team may even include a combination of church and community members.

A project manager in the business world makes a commitment to achieve a project's objective while meeting a promised timeline without using more money or other resources than originally allocated. Although the role of the project manager in a church, social, or not-for-profit setting may differ in some ways from that of a manager in the business world, there are many similarities. Following are nine characteristics of a project manager in a business organization that also apply to the role of a project manager in a church setting:

1. **An organizer:** capacity to understand, plan, and coordinate efforts and resources to meet the objectives

2. **A strategist:** able to set clear long- and short-term objectives, keeping these in mind together with the reasons for the project's existence

3. **A motivator:** skills and attitudes enabling him or her to motivate and commit people to the project or to participate in it (workers, volunteers, young people)

4. **A fund-raiser:** knowledge and confidence to apply for funds to administer and account for them with integrity and competence

5. **An activist:** someone able to spot initiatives and to organize ideas into meaningful Christian actions with clear values evolving over time

6. **A visionary:** someone able to imagine social good innovation and change

7. **A community worker:** particular concern for the affairs of the community or church organization he or she is involved in

8. **A social worker:** capable of caring for people without replacing them (i.e., instilling in them the motivation and confidence to take part in shaping their own future and realizing their projects)

9. **A teacher and a learner:** capable of empowering people while at the same time being able to learn from the experiences and use that knowledge for the church, project, or community—monitoring and evaluating a process in relation to the objectives, changing plans, and ultimately achieving those objectives in relation to the circumstances.[14]

Furthermore, within the secular organization, the project manager is driven by company values, department objectives and norms, and even personal gain. The work of the church is different. A project manager in a church is a leader within a spiritual context. From a Christian perspective, considering scriptural guidance when preparing for or serving as a leader is imperative. Gregory Ingram, a bishop in the African Methodist Episcopal Church, gives emphasis to this point: "Leaders in the church serve because they have been called to do so; therefore, it is that they are in right relationship with God, through Jesus Christ, in order to worthily execute their service."[15]

In summary, a project manager is an influential factor in project execution and success. As the leader, she or he is responsible for leading the project team in planning, organizing, monitoring, and controlling the project activities in order to accomplish the project requirements in support of a broader ministry for Christ. Since project managers in this context operate in the church, they must be called and led by God in performing their work. The church project manager is therefore like the choir director of a large choir, making sure that each section sings its part at the right time in the right way, and that all perform together in melodious harmony.

NOTES

1. H. Kerzner, *Project Management: A Systems Approach to Planning, Scheduling, and Controlling* (Hoboken, NJ: John Wiley and Sons, 2009), 956.

2. J. Kouzes and B. Posner, *The Leadership Challenge* (San Francisco: Jossey-Bass, 2002), 18.

3. L. M. Russell, *The Future of Partnership* (Philadelphia: Westminster, 1979), 72.

4. W. R. Duncan, *A Guide to the Project Management Book of Knowledge* (Upper Darby, PA: Project Management Institute, 1996), 4.

5. Adapted from Project Management T-Kit No. 3, Council of Europe and European Commission, November 2000, p. 31, http://pjp-eu.coe.int/documents/1017981/1667915/tkit3.pdf/63828fe8-4022-4944-9459-32ac0c8b6fbf.

6. T. Kloppenborg, A. Shriberg, and J. Venkatraman, *Project Leadership, The Project Management Essential Library* (Tysons Corner, VA: Management Concepts, 2003), 18.

7. Adapted from Jason Westland, *The Project Management Life Cycle: A Complete Step-by-Step Methodology for Initiating, Planning, Executing and Closing a Project Successfully* (Philadelphia: Kogan Page, 2007), 3–7.

8. A. Lester, *Project Management, Planning and Control* (Waltham, MA: Butterworth-Heinemann, 2014), 7.

9. J. R. Meredith and S. Mantel, *Project Management: A Managerial Approach* (Hoboken, NJ: John Wiley and Sons, 2009), 2.

10. Ibid., 1–2.

11. A. T. Cobb, *Leading Project Teams: An Introduction to the Basics of Project Management* (Thousand Oaks, CA: Sage, 2006), 18.

12. P. C. Dinsmore, *Human Factors in Project Management* (New York: AMACOM, 1990), 40.

13. "Vince Lombardi Quotes," Vince Lombardi, attributed, Iacocca, http://www.notable-quotes.com/l/lombardi_vince.html; accessed December 29, 2016.

14. Project Management T-Kit No. 3, 39.

15. G. Ingram, *Equipping the Saints for Service* (Nashville: African Methodist Epicopal Church Publishing House, 2002), 6.

CHAPTER 3

→

A Theological Foundation for Project Management

Over the past fifty years or so, project management has been applied in varying settings in organizations of all sizes. It is a proven concept. Nonetheless, it is critical that we evaluate its application in the church through the lens of Scripture. In this chapter, I will look to scriptural guidance in support of the application of project management and leadership discipline in the church.

We can classify a church or congregation as a nonprofit service organization led by Christ that is organized and mandated to make disciples for Christ, and that is to provide ministerial service in the name of Christ. Key to this classification is the term *Christian organization.* Any successful organization must have an effective leadership and management function.[1] And any church organization leadership function must have God as the foundation for leadership. As Scripture says, "We are not saying that we can do this work ourselves. It is God who makes us able to do all that we do. He made us able to be servants of a new agreement from himself to his people" (2 Corinthians 3:5-6, NCV).

A number of organizations could benefit by applying project management, be they profit- or service-mission driven. "Although often used in construction and technology industries, basic project management could readily be applied to small, non-technical activities as well, including arts and social sciences."[2] In support of this point, here is an example from a human services perspective:

> Health, Education, and Welfare (HEW) performs social work largely on the basis of grants through states and local agencies. Associated with each grant are time, cost, and performance requirements of the funding agencies. In essence, each grant results in a project or projects—to which the concepts of project management apply.
>
> When an advertising firm conducts a promotional campaign it utilizes the support of marketing, research, accounting, graphics, sales, and other units. Several projects are usually underway at any given time, each in a different state of its life cycle. These campaigns are similar to the projects . . . in other industries that commonly practice project management.
>
> A good deal of work performed in education development can be considered project work. Like HEW, much of this work is funded by grants with target goals and cost and time constraints. Also, the work requires coordination among many educators and researchers—a task for which project management is ideally suited.[3]

So with the foundation laid that project management is part of the broader discipline of management, and that project management should be applicable even to organizations such as the church, let us now look to Scripture for guidance.

Leadership Philosophy

Leadership philosophy from a biblical perspective requires that when defining a project's purpose or mission, we must have a dream and a vision—for example, Proverbs 29:18 and Joel 2:28.[4] Furthermore, the apostle Paul speaks to the church at Ephesus, saying that God provides different roles, responsibilities, and functions in the church "for the equipping of the saints for the work of ministry, for the edifying of the body of Christ" (Ephesians 4:12, NKJV). Each project can be viewed as a set of tools that can be used by lay and clerical leaders in managing God's work in ministry-related projects.

Paul continues this emphasis as he mentors Titus, a young preacher and church leader. Paul tells Titus repeatedly to instruct the people of God about the importance of preparing to do the work of Christ and the church: "Remind them . . . to be ready for every good work" (Titus 3:1, NKJV). Being ready to do good work for the church and the Lord requires preparation and tools. Project management is a tool set that can assist in accomplishing a productive result from the work.

In any organization, including the church, the project manager is the leader of the team charged with executing the project management concept. He therefore must make sure the project team understands the vision, knows the purpose, stays focused on the purpose, and has internalized this purpose as his or her own in order to drive success. The leader must also lead in a way that is consistent with Scripture. Further, in context of the church, any leader—project manager or pastor—must lead knowing that the ultimate leader is God and seeking God's guidance as a requirement for laying a Christian foundation for success. The Gospel writer Matthew reminds leaders to "seek ye first the kingdom of God, and his righteousness; and all these things shall be added unto you" (Matthew 6:33, KJV).

Scripture-Focused Leadership

Andrew Clark, whose research has focused on the use of secular leadership tools in the local church, further emphasizes the importance of Scripture-focused leadership, employing the church at Corinth as an example.

> One of Paul's chief concerns with the Corinthians in 1 Corinthians 1–6 is to deal with the issue of leadership within the Christian community. This question is addressed directly at a number of points in the early chapters of the epistle, and it has become clear that Paul's own assessment of the situation is that within the church are those who have derived their view of leadership from the surrounding Greco-Roman society.
>
> Paul confronts this situation on two fronts: He demonstrates the inappropriateness of secular leadership models within the Christian church; and secondly, he presents his own definition of true Christian leadership.
>
> In redefining for the Corinthians the true nature of Christian leadership, Paul's careful use of language is of considerable importance. He adopts images of leadership which erode the secular perception of how leaders should view themselves, and he patiently uses the rhetorical device of covert allusion, itself a device of secular leaders, in order to make plain to the Corinthians the nature of their leading.
>
> Paul also refers the Corinthians to the good examples of Christian leadership they have encountered. Principally he reminds them of his own behavior whilst working among them.[5]

The Old Testament story of Nehemiah and his leadership of rebuilding of the walls of Jerusalem provides a biblical example of project management. The Christian leadership applied in this story not only highlights Nehemiah's leadership but also provides guidance for leaders today when they face challenges while undertaking various projects in the local church. Here I will highlight some key components of project management and responsibilities of the project manager found in this Scripture.

The rebuilding of the Jerusalem wall project began when Nehemiah heard about the depressed conditions in the city. A report from a visitor to the city reported that the walls had fallen and the gates of Jerusalem were in ruins. As a result, Nehemiah was concerned that the city was not in a position of safety. So when he heard this report, he responded by praying for the Holy Spirit's guidance concerning a restoration project endeavor. Here is how the project came together.

Look for the Community Need and Get Leadership Support

Nehemiah took the opportunity to share his concern and the need for the project in a meeting with the king. Scripture says, "Then the king said to me, 'What do you request?' So I prayed to the God of heaven. And I said to the king, 'If it pleases the king, and if your servant has found favor in your sight, I ask that you send me to Judah, to the city of my fathers' tombs, that I may rebuild it'" (Nehemiah 2:4-5, NKJV). Nehemiah's request was approved, providing key leadership support and sponsorship for the project. He was now ready to start project planning.

Gather Knowledge

As noted, the project idea was based on a report that was shared with Nehemiah. Now that the project was supported by the king, it became beneficial to get first-hand knowledge of the situation to define the full scope of what needed to be done. Therefore Nehemiah researched conditions on site for himself. Scripture says, "Then I arose in the night, I and a few men with me; I told no one what my God had put in my heart to do at Jerusalem" (Nehemiah 2:12, NKJV).

Build a Team to Achieve and Execute the Project

By referring to Nehemiah 2:17-18, we see how Nehemiah gathered the people together and shared his project idea (rebuilding the walls). From a project management perspective, he was identifying the problem that needed to be solved. Specifically he said to them, "Come and let us build the wall of Jerusalem, that we may no longer be a reproach" (v. 17, NKJV).

Another key component of project team building is team member involvement. We see this emphasis on the part of Nehemiah as he encouraged the people to identify resources already available to complete the project. He then garnered their support and secured their commitment to work on the project, and they responded by saying: "'Let us rise up and build.' Then they set their hearts to this good work" (v. 18, NKJV).

Develop a Contingency Plan for Risks and Conflict

In the execution of any project, conflicts, criticism, and other issues will likely come up, threatening to derail the effort. It is best to plan for these challenges up-front. This was Nehemiah's situation, and as we read in Scripture, he dealt with his circumstances and, at the same time, remained confident in the mission God had given him. "But when Sanballat the Horonite, Tobiah the Ammonite official, and Geshem the Arab heard of it, they laughed at us and despised us, and said, 'What is this thing that you are doing? Will you rebel against the king?' So I answered them, and said to them, 'The God of heaven Himself will prosper us; therefore we His servants will arise and build, but you have no heritage or right or memorial in Jerusalem'" (Nehemiah 2:19-20, NKJV).

Divide the Work into Manageable Tasks

As we saw in verses 17-18 where Nehemiah put together a project team, the added requirement is to define who does what task and when. (This is called project planning, which we will talk more about in a future chapter.) Nehemiah 3:1-32 tells us that he divided the work into manageable tasks and assigned specific responsibilities to members of his team based on their skills. They got to work, monitored progress, and made changes and adjustments as needed, as indicated in events that occurred in Nehemiah 4:8-9.

Manage Human Resource Issues

Projects are about people working together. Invariably people-related conflicts (often related to lack of information or misunderstandings) need to be addressed. This is the norm today just as it was in Nehemiah's day. When these types of situations came up, he made adjustments. Nehemiah 5:1-13 summarizes Nehemiah's experience:

> A great protest was mounted by the people, including the wives, against their fellow Jews. Some said, "We have big families, and we need food just to survive."
>
> Others said, "We're having to mortgage our fields and vineyards and homes to get enough grain to keep from starving."
>
> And others said, "We're having to borrow money to pay the royal tax on our fields and vineyards. Look: We're the same flesh and blood as our brothers here; our children are just as good as theirs. Yet here we are having to sell our children off as slaves—some of our daughters have already been sold—and we can't do anything about it because our fields and vineyards are owned by somebody else."
>
> I got really angry when I heard their protest and complaints. After thinking it over, I called the nobles and officials on the carpet. I said, "Each one of you is gouging his brother."
>
> Then I called a big meeting to deal with them. I told them, "We did everything we could to buy back our Jewish brothers who had to sell themselves as slaves to foreigners. And now

you're selling these same brothers back into debt slavery! Does that mean that we have to buy them back again?"

They said nothing. What could they say?

"What you're doing is wrong. Is there no fear of God left in you? Don't you care what the nations around here, our enemies, think of you?" . . .

They said, "We won't make any more demands on them. We'll do everything you say."

Then I called the priests together and made them promise to keep their word. . . .

Everyone gave a wholehearted "Yes, we'll do it!" and praised GOD. And the people did what they promised. (MSG, adapted)

In summary, Nehemiah and his team stuck to the project until it was completed. In addition, they were able to manage through all the distractions and conflicts. "So the wall was finished on the twenty-fifth day of Elul, in fifty-two days" (Nehemiah 6:15).

The Old Testament book of Nehemiah also provides important insight into the role of the project manager as a people leader, writes Chuck Swindoll, pastor, author, and former president of Dallas Theological Seminary:

If you think about the characteristics of Nehemiah's leadership revealed in this chapter, you will find a single theme threaded throughout: unselfishness. Unconcerned about having his name in lights, Nehemiah stepped aside and strengthened the overall project with fresh reinforcements—people like Ezra who was better than he in handling of the Scripture. And as Ezra did his job, Nehemiah stood among the people applying the truth that was proclaimed. It posed no problem for him to step aside and have his wall project virtually ignored because a far more significant activity was taking place among the people. Why? His mind-set was unselfish.[6]

The Scripture is definitive about the criticality of leadership in the context of the church and its ministries. Further, associated leadership functions, such as project management, should be rooted in Christian practice and faith. When management and leadership principles are applied in the church, there is no substitute for the Scriptures being the document of governance. Project management, too, must be carried out in Christlike love.

Implications for Ministry

The essence of project management is that it is a concept and a set of tools that can be used in the effective leadership of an organization. Project management, though primarily used in the corporate arena, can add value to the management and leadership structure of organizations such as the church. The theological foundation for this conclusion is found in Ephesians 4:12 in that God gave different roles, responsibilities, and functions in the church "for the equipping of the saints for the work of ministry, for the edifying of the body of Christ" (NKJV). Project management can be viewed as a set of tools that can be used by lay and pastoral leaders for managing God's work in ministerial related projects.

Project management has been successfully used in such Christian ministries as Habitat for Humanity International. The Habitat experience and lessons learned could add insight for such projects in many church and ministry plans as the renovation of a church parsonage, the expansion of a sanctuary, the move to a recently purchased sanctuary in a different neighborhood, and the upgrade of a church kitchen. Yet more spiritual activities can be managed as projects too. Typical projects in this category include designing and implementing an evangelism program when a congregation relocates to a new neighborhood, adding a Girl Scout ministry to the Christian education program, initiating a missions project in support of the local homeless shelter, conducting an annual community dinner for the homeless on Thanksgiving, and planning a Bible study, vacation Bible school, or a church marketing and outreach strategy to increase community participation—just to name a few.

Project management tools can enable the congregation to provide and deliver services and ministries more efficiently by providing a road map for lay leaders that is easily followed and leads to project completion. Regardless of whether the church is a large organization or an auxiliary within the church organization, and regardless of scope, project size, or complexity, all projects go through the same series of stages. And with a project manager who understands and pays attention to these related details, the church will be in a better position to achieve a successful project outcome.

Furthermore, as technology project managers Ron Wallace and Wayne Halverson emphasize, along with the valuable team structure of project management, projects provide a structured environment for people to work together, thereby promoting teamwork and communication across the total organization.[7] Such a productive team environment helps to furnish a positive volunteer experience, which in turn is important to motivating future participation and commitment.

Church members bring with them a vast set of experiences and commitment that at times goes untapped. And many either have leadership experience through their work or have the potential for leadership. The Habitat for Humanity experience confirms that its application of project management in its Christian ministry has proved to be a vehicle for providing learning opportunities for those individuals who not only enjoy helping the community, but also desire to learn something new.[8] Project management not only provides learning through project execution; but for those who have leadership experience or interest, it can provide a unique opportunity for leadership learning with a Christian perspective. Lovett H. Weems Jr., professor of church leadership at Wesley Theological Seminary, provides insight into the fundamental nature of leadership in a church-based project management context: "Leadership, like other work of the people of faith, depends upon the vigorous and responsible use of the talents God has given to each of us. It depends upon the work of the Spirit weaving those talents into a rich tapestry. It is the marvelous and mysterious working of God through our lives and work that we call grace. Leadership is a gift from God, confirmed by the church, for the service of others and the upbuilding of the body of Christ."[9]

In conclusion, there is a solid theological base that supports the theory that project management concepts can add value to ministry effectiveness as we equip the saints for the work of ministry, for the edifying of the body of Christ (Ephesians 4:11-13). Project management can be a set of tools that can be used by church leaders in managing God's work in ministry-related projects.

NOTES

1. L. H. Weems, *Church Leadership: Vision, Team, Culture and Integrity* (Nashville: Abingdon, 1993), 15.

2. J. M. Nicholas and H. Steyn, *Project Management for Business, Engineering, and Technology: Principles and Practices* (Burlington, MA: Elsevier, 2008), 15.

3. J. R. Adams, S. E.https://www.google.com/search?tbo=p&tbm=bks&q=inauthor:%22John+R.+Adams%22 Barndt, and M. D. Martin, *Managing by Project Management* (Dayton, OH: Universal Technology, 1979), 12–13.

4. R. H. Migliore, R. E. Stevens, and D. L. Loudon, *Church and Ministry Strategic Planning: From Concept to Success* (Binghamton, NY: Haworth, 1994), 24.

5. A. D. Clark, *Secular and Christian Leadership in Corinth: A Socio-Historical and Exegetical Study of 1 Corinthians 1–6* (Leiden: E. J. Brill, 1993), 126–27.

6. C. R. Swindoll, *Hand Me Another Brick* (Nashville: Word, 1998), 134.

7. R. Wallace and W. Halverson, "Project Management: A Critical Success Factor or a Management Fad?," *Industrial Engineering*, April 1992, 48–50.

8. E. Verzuh, *The Fast Forward MBA in Project Management* (Hoboken, NJ: John Wiley and Sons, 2008), 294.

9. Weems, *Church Leadership*, 17.

PART TWO

How to Apply Project Management in the Church

CHAPTER 4

➤

Doing Projects in the Church
CHURCH PROJECT
INSPIRATION AND INITIATION

This chapter, and those that follow, will look at the process for implementing the project management concept in the church.

The first step in project management is *project initiation*. Project initiation starts with an idea—and more specifically, with *divine inspiration*. This is where God has given you or the congregation an idea for meeting a need of the church or community you serve—something like vacation Bible school for the coming year, a new food pantry, a young adult Sunday school program, or parsonage renovations. This list of project ideas could be much longer, but the key thing to remember in church project management is that any idea for a project needs to be inspired by the Holy Spirit.

Bishop Mark J. Webb, prelate of the Upper New York Conference of the United Methodist Church, provided a good example in this regard when he said that as followers of Christ, we must "see with Jesus' eyes, we must feel with the heart of Jesus, who was burdened and broken over the spiritual condition of people."[1] When we do this, God will inspire the church with projects that will address the needs of people in the community and the church.

Projects done in the secular arena are typically for the benefit of an organization. For example, they may boost profits or enhance market advantage. They are inward-focused. Not so for churches. Our projects are intentionally outward-focused, and when we focus on service and ministry, both the community and the local congregation benefit.

The best way to ensure that a project idea starts with God's inspiration is to seek God's will in prayer. Whether the idea is generated through an individual church member, an existing committee such as the trustee board, the pastor or one of the ministers, or the administrative board that plans ministries (strategic planning) for the coming year, let the Lord, not personal ego, be your inspiration for any church project idea. Remember, "in every situation let your petitions be made known to God through prayers and requests, with thanksgiving" (Philippians 4:6, ISV). Figure 4A is a template that can be used for guiding your process of church project idea generation. This template can also be used in conjunction with ministry team brainstorming to generate project ideas that are action plans from a church's strategic plan implementation.)

Because you will at some time in the future need to communicate this idea to others, such as individuals who serve on the project team, the administrative board, or the congregation as a whole, it will be good to state the project idea in the form of a problem you are trying to solve or an objective you are trying to achieve. When you write your objective statement, it should be SMART:

- ▶ Specific
- ▶ Measurable

FIGURE 4A

Church Project Idea Development Work Sheet

Instructions: Your ministry team can use this template to develop ideas for ministry projects. With as much detail as possible, complete this template to describe your thoughts about your church project idea. (A separate sheet can be used for each project idea.)

What Scripture or life experience has inspired this project idea?
What do you feel called to do (goal statement)?
Why is it important (what is the significance) to the ministry of the church?
Proposed Objectives 1. 2.
Activities / methodology / approach
Expected outcomes
Expected partners / collaborators
Project timing and cost

- ► Achievable
- ► Relevant
- ► Timely[2]

Here are some examples of church project objectives:

- ► Increase the number of college scholarships available to youth in the community by introducing three new scholarships for students to apply for in 2018. Each scholarship awarded will be a minimum of $1,000.

- ► Implement a Thanksgiving dinner for the homeless at the community center, serving two hundred people, on November 22, 2018.

- ► Implement a strategy for making new disciples by introducing small groups (one focused on men, one on teens, and one on women), with each kicking off by May 1, 2018.

Now that God has inspired a project idea, the next step is to *get initial buy-in*. This is especially important if the idea comes through an individual prior to meeting with your committee, pastor, or church board. Note that buy-in is not final approval. By getting initial buy-in, you are able to vet the idea and get additional input that may strengthen the objective God has inspired. This initial buy-in process can be a one-on-one meeting (with an influential lay leader or the pastor or staff minister), or it may be a review and presentation at the next committee meeting.

One of the best ways to succeed in this step is to *prepare a project charter*. The charter is your first step in documenting an idea and planning for a future project plan. A project charter is a critical component for church project initiation and planning because it describes your project and captures initial details that will be used in planning and execution. You will refer to this vital one-page document throughout the life of the project.

Inspiration for your project may have come to you through service, devotions, prayer, worship, or Scripture reading. So in addition to details such as the church name, date of proposal, project due date, and name of the project and the project manager, the charter should also include the following:

► **Biblical inspiration.** Anchor the project in a scriptural theme or text. This helps the team and the leader keep focused on the fact that the project is for the Lord and that we need to become less concerned with church work and more concerned with kingdom work. For example, a church putting on a dinner that focuses on fund raising only, and not purposely using this as an opportunity to make new disciples for Christ, is missing an opportunity for kingdom building.

► **Project objective.** Every project needs a clearly stated goal or purpose. Develop a statement that describes the scope needed to achieve the planned benefits of the project. This statement should be SMART. (See pages 34 and 36 to review SMART goals.) Objectives are at times referred to as deliverables. The focus is to produce or deliver a ministry or service, either to the church who sponsors the project or to the group of people being served. Examples of deliverables are (1) put on the 2018 vacation Bible school, (2) remodel the parsonage for the new pastor who arrives July 1, (3) establish a small group for youth by year's end, and (4) host a community breakfast for those in need on the day prior to Thanksgiving.

► **Ministry needs summary.** Briefly describe the gap in the community where you serve or the need for ministry you see in your local church that begs for this project to be implemented.

▶ **Proposed budget.** Estimate the required funding necessary to do the project. For example, if the project is to upgrade the church audio and video system, a budget of $10,000 might be estimated to cover the cost to buy new equipment, hire an installer, buy supplies such as cables and connectors, and build and install an equipment booth.

▶ **Project resources and requirements.** List what all the project team needs to achieve the objective (e.g., specific people who can make a contribution or general skill sets needed). This is preliminary, so you don't need individual commitments yet.

▶ **Project milestones.** Highlight significant events in the project that let you know you are on schedule (e.g., if hosting a Thanksgiving dinner for the homeless, a key milestone could be "food is delivered").

▶ **Success criteria.** Establish measures or criteria for how you will know to what degree you achieved your objective. These may be assessments that you secure only after the project is complete (e.g., a survey of participants, a final count of registrations, the total funds raised). So the charter should allow for a target measure as well as the actual measure achieved.

▶ **Actual date of project completion.** The target date should be included as part of your SMART goal under "Project Objectives" or separately under "Project Due Date." The actual date will be a valuable part of the post-project evaluation.

As you can see in figure 4B, the project charter provides a summary of what the project intends to address.

FIGURE 4B
Church Project Charter

Church Name: City Baptist Church	**Date:** August 17, 2017
Project Name: Camp Experience for Community Kids	**Project Manager:** Alexandra Doe

Biblical Inspiration
In reading Psalm 23:2-3, I was reminded of summer church camp when growing up—the outdoors, the greenery, the beauty of the earth. Some kids have never been to camp.

Project Objective
Establish fund-raising effort to raise $2,000 by May 31, 2018, to fund 8 children (ages 10–13; 4 boys and 4 girls) to attend Camp Casowasco for two weeks during the summer of 2018

Ministry Needs Summary
Many kids in our neighborhood have never been out in nature or been to camp. During the summer they have limited activities. Because local families have limited financial resources and limited access to green spaces, and because there is also a need for Christian outreach and faith formation for school-aged children, this project has the potential to meet several needs in our community.

Proposed Budget: $300.00	**Project Due Date:** July 8, 2018

Project Milestones
1. Confirmed group of 8 kids, ages 10–13, who can go to camp (with parental permission)
2. Fund-raising completed
3. Transportation plan confirmed
4. Commitment from at least 2 adult chaperones

Success Criteria	**Actual Result**
1. Achieve fund-raising goal of $2,000 plus 25 percent	1. Fund-raising:
2. Survey of children and parents indicates positive experience; goal 85 percent	2. Positive survey responses:

Actual Date of Project Completion:

Notes/Comments: *(Add any notes that might be helpful during planning or execution of the project; could also include key feedback from the leadership board.)*

Now that you have a project charter, it is time to meet with the appropriate church leadership to initiate approval discussions. Only then can you proceed with the project and start more detailed project planning. Based on past communication during the initial buy-in stage, determine how best to secure the necessary approvals. Again, this can be a one-on-one meeting, a review at the next committee meeting, a formal pitch to the leadership board, or a presentation for vote at a congregational meeting—or some process that includes more than one of these forums. You may want to include the project charter when presenting to a larger forum. Once your project is approved, you are ready to begin the next phase—church project planning.

NOTES

1. Comment made by Bishop Mark J. Webb, presiding prelate of the Upper New York Annual Conference of the United Methodist Church, at the 2015 session of the Annual Conference.

2. The acronym SMART as a mnemonic device is most commonly attributed to author and business consultant Peter F. Drucker, in his 1954 book, *The Practice of Management*.

CHAPTER 5

➤

Church Project Planning

You may have heard the old adage "If you fail to plan, you plan to fail." In a perfect world, every church project would achieve its objective, meet the planned time of execution, and be within budget (or better yet, under budget). The purpose of church project management is to work toward achieving that aim, and to do that, you need a documented plan. Thus the planning phase of your church project must be viewed as critical, and sufficient time must be allotted to plan. By having a documented plan, the church and church leadership are in a better position to measure success (or failure) against what was envisioned.

Think about these scenarios. Have you ever been working on a project at church (or on your job, for that matter) when the project showed signs of disorganization and you started to wonder if the team would achieve its objective? Or have you been part of a project where everyone worked in a silo and no one seemed to know what the rest of the team was doing? What about team members who only wanted to do their part and disregarded how their work fit with the work of others? Even worse is when a team has its regular meeting but no one knows what is going on or the criticality of his or her role in the success of the project.

Situations similar to these scenarios point to a lack of a plan and potential indications that church project failure is possible. None of us wants that, yet project management experts highlight that "lack of a solid project plan" is a key reason for project failure.[1] Thus every church project needs to have a documented project plan.

Who Does the Work of Planning?

Church projects are executed by a project manager and a project team. Here are some basics about the project manager and the project team:

▶ Every project must have a project manager.

▶ The primary aim of the project manager is to achieve the results inspired by God and the congregation (i.e., the objective of the project).

▶ The role the project manager plays is that of team leader and facilitator (not micromanager).

Concerning the project manager being a leader and a facilitator of the project team, Vance Packard, noted journalist and author of *The Hidden Persuaders*, points out, "Leadership is the art of getting others to *want* to do something that you believe should be done." Project management authorities also highlight that without good leadership, projects tend to get minimal results. Keep in mind these key thoughts on the role of project manager:

▶ A project manager is the person responsible for leading a project from its inception to planning, execution, and managing of people, resources, and the entire scope of the project, including schedule, cost, and quality of the ministry implementation.

► The project manager must have the self-discipline needed for creating clear and attainable objectives and for seeing them through to successful completion.

► In the church context, a project manager may be an appointee or a volunteer, but it is important to look for someone with a passion for the ministry the project is seeking to address.[2]

The bottom line: the role of the project manager is critical.

The project team executes the project plans. It is not the role of the project manager to do all of the tasks or produce whatever concrete outcomes are called for in the project plan. The project manager must avoid the attitude that the best way to get something done is to do it yourself. Church project team members, working closely together, are responsible for accomplishing tasks and generating deliverables as documented in the project plan. All of this is accomplished under the leadership of the project manager. Therefore, achieving the project objectives, schedule, and cost constraints results from the synergy of an effective project team and project manager.

With this foundation for church project leadership and team building, it is the joint role of the team and the project manager to plan and execute the project. Susanne Madsen, writing on the *PM Perspectives* blog, emphasizes this point:

> Traditionally it has been the project manager's responsibility to plan the project—and for the most part that is still the case. But in recent years there has been an increased recognition of the importance of collaborative planning. The project manager is no longer expected to do it all in isolation. In fact there is a growing pressure from the team to be involved—and with good reason. Not only will the quality of the plan improve when the team is involved. It will also increase commitment and promote a shared sense of ownership, which are significant bonuses.[3]

One final thought concerning project managers is, what are the roles of the pastor and the administrative boards of the church? In some circles, since the pastor is often viewed as the central leader in the church, the congregation may assume the pastor will be the project manager. This is typically not the case. The senior pastor (or designated pastoral staff member, depending on the size of the church) has an equally critical role that is appropriate to play, and that is the role of "champion."

From a church project management perspective, the champion takes on the burden of ensuring that the congregation and those involved, such as the project team and the administrative board, are supportive and behind the ultimate success of the project. The church project champion is responsible to do the following:

▶ Serve as an advocate for the project, including as a sounding board and confidant to the project manager.

▶ Work with the project team to ensure that the vision for the project is successfully translated into the requirements and tasks to achieve the objective.

▶ Monitor team activities, looking for best practices that can be shared with future projects.

▶ Identify and eliminate obstacles that may threaten a project's viability within the church.

▶ Collaborate with the administrative board to work through priority issues when conflicts arise that impact church strategy.

▶ Advise on communication from the project managers to ensure timely updates to the congregation and administrative board.

▶ Act as the conduit within the church to ensure appropriate allocation and organization of resources (e.g., volunteers and appropriate funding) to facilitate the successful completion, implementation, and adoption of the project.

Yes, the pastor has an important role in church project management. With the pastor in the role of champion, the project team has a person to go to with questions, needs, and even conflicts that may arise. This is important in any organization that has a strong foundation in leadership of people.

The congregation's main administrative board, be it deacon board, leadership team, or executive council, has an important advisory or steering role, especially when the congregation is taking on multiple projects in a particular year. This "advisory committee" will provide high-level input and offer guidance when priority calls need to be made or when conflicts arise that have an impact on church strategy; help supply resource needs—for example, church volunteers, community resources, and appropriate funding; and help with communication to the broader congregation and community.

Team Organization

With a clear understanding of the role of the project team, it is now time to start preparing a plan for the project resource requirements so you can ultimately determine whom you will need to ask to serve on the project team. For this part of church project planning, the use of a "role and responsibility matrix" is effective (see fig. 5A). The role and responsibility matrix is comprised of a list of each type of resource, along with what tasks volunteers will be expected to do to achieve the objective. Initially, this matrix is prepared by the project manager. Because at this stage the matrix is preliminary, the focus is on role and responsibility, not on specific names of individuals who will fill the role.

This step is critical in that it provides information about what work is needed when you are ready to solicit volunteers for the project. The matrix then becomes a communication tool. By having it in writing, along with the project charter, volunteers you recruit to be on the team will have a better understanding of their responsibilities and how their roles might be fulfilled. Once you have organized the full complement of volunteers, this preliminary role and responsibility matrix should be reviewed in an early team meeting so that everyone on the team is knowledgeable about one another's roles.

Here is an example of how the role and responsibility matrix is used. For reference purposes, let us say the objective of a project is to "hold a swiss steak dinner that can serve approximately 150, on August 17, 2017, to raise $800 to contribute to the City Children's Shelter." The church administrative board and pastor have approved the project, and you as the church project manager have developed an initial draft of the project charter. You now need to determine the roles and responsibilities necessary so that the project can seek volunteers to make up the project team. Figure 5A provides an example of how you would define these roles using a matrix template. The "Role" column is where you define what jobs are required to execute the event. Again, the focus here is on roles and responsibilities only, not names of people. You will add names later.

As noted above, this exercise gives you a written view of what is needed to execute your project. It is still preliminary and may be only as complete as the information you currently have. But it is your starting point, and you will use it to refine your project plan later.

Communication

Now that you have a preliminary role and responsibility matrix, it is time to communicate with appropriate church leadership (e.g., pastor as champion, chair of deacon board). This communication does not need to happen at a formal church committee

Role and Responsibility Matrix

Project Name: Children's Shelter Dinner   **Target Date:** 8/17/17
Document Revision Date: January 25, 2017   **Project Manager:** Jane Doe

Role	Responsibility	Name
Project Champion	• Provide advice to project manager. • Give advice on suggested team members. • Assist with conflict resolution.	
Advisory Board (Board of Deacons)	• Provide high-level input. • Approve budget. • Prayer/look for discipleship opportunities	
Project Manager	• Manage project activities. • Lead team to achieve objectives, schedule, and budget. • Coordinate selection of team members.	
Menu Planning and Food Preparation	• Recommend menu. • Coordinate food preparation plan. • Determine plan for cooks.	
Servers/Greeters	• Determine service plan—buffet style or serve at tables. • Refill drinks.	
Dining Hall Setup and Cleanup	• Set up tables and chairs. • Place tablecloths. • Be prepared to clean spills. • Clean up dining hall after event.	
Cooks	• Cook food per menu planning and food prep plan.	
Publicity	• Write press release for newspaper. • Get event posted on church website and Facebook site. • Contact TV station. • Provide communication for internal church publications.	
Ticket Collection and Sales at Door	• Determine how many people need to be at the door(s) to sell tickets and collect presold tickets.	
Ticket Sales	• Organize team to sell tickets. • Define ticket sales and accounting plan. • Prepare sales and collection account summary for church treasurer.	

meeting. Based on your own church's communication practices, determine how best to do this. This could be a one-on-one meeting, a phone conference, a review at the next committee meeting, or something else. At this stage, the primary purpose of communication is to get additional feedback as you feel it is necessary. And after you have received feedback, refine the matrix based on those inputs. (Note that I have included a date of revision of the matrix template. Depending on the complexity of your project, it is good to be able to edit your electronic documents as you go.)

Recruitment

It is now time to solicit volunteers for the project team. Here are some important considerations for planning the people resource component of a church project.

First, emphasize that the project you are working on is in the context of the church. A church is Christ-centered. As Christian educator Robert Verlarde points out, the church "involves edifying believers, but also nurturing, building up or helping believers to mature in Christ. To this end, churches are tasked with a variety of ministries such as Bible study, continuing education in related areas, praying for one another, acts of genuine hospitality and more."[4] Yet we also have an evangelism component, as we are taught in Matthew 28:19 to go and make disciples in the community and the world. Therefore the church is to minister to both the congregation and the local community. The congregation must be seen as synergistic to the community, as the prophet Isaiah instructs us: "The Spirit of God is on us, because God anointed us to preach good news, and to comfort all who mourn, and to care for the needs of all" (Isaiah 61:1-7, condensed and paraphrased).

With this in mind, when it comes time to gather project team members, start with members of the church, because often the church will be the sponsoring organization for the project. Look for persons who have skills required by the role and responsibility matrix, as well as those who have a passion for the project. When resources within the church are limited or community resources will add value to achieving the project objective, by all means reach out to people and agencies in the community for support.

For example, our congregation, the Westside United Methodist Church, in Elmira, New York, is in its second year of doing a project called Family FunFest, where we focus on bringing community members together for fun, fellowship, food, and sharing the Word of God. When the project team met to plan requirements, one of the desired ministries in the event was to make sure anyone who did not have a Bible could be given one. One of our church members is affiliated with Gideons International, and he was able to get some Gideons members to come and work with the church to distribute Bibles and support sharing the Good News.[5]

A second consideration for securing project team members is to understand the implications of these team members being volunteers. Projects in secular organizations, for instance, a machinery company, will assign resources based on market profit-and-loss considerations. The project becomes a part of the team members' job responsibility, and therefore the work supports their livelihood. In that context, the team members may or may not have a passion for the project (i.e., maybe they wanted to work on another project, but for whatever reason, this was the one that was the priority for the organization at the time). Nevertheless, because this is "part of the job," earning a livelihood becomes a key driving force.

Whereas project team members in a for-profit corporation or government agency may desire to work on a specific project for career growth and development (think promotion, a raise, or positioning oneself for a longer-term career opportunity), a completely different dynamic is at play for church project team members.

Project team members in the church are typically volunteers, and volunteers generally have a different motivation for participating than do paid workers. Susan J. Ellis, president of Energize, Inc., a training, consulting, and publishing firm specializing in volunteerism, points out that the impetus to volunteer can come from a large number of motives, including to feel needed, to make new friends, to explore a career, to help someone, for therapy, to gain leadership skills, to keep busy, for recognition, or to donate professional skills.[6] Dr. Thomas Wolfe, former Harvard professor and leadership consultant, points out in his *Managing a Nonprofit Organization in the Twenty-First Century* that it is important for those leading volunteers, including project managers, to understand volunteer needs and to understand how a particular task or project can fulfill those needs.[7] Thus a project manager must be sensitive and considerate in managing project team members. To not do so risks project success as well as team synergy, as Wolfe affirms: "A volunteer wants meaningful responsibility and wants to be taken seriously. The minute we take a volunteer for granted, we are in trouble."[8]

Keep this advice in mind as you solicit volunteers to serve on the church project team:

▶ Review and gain clarity on the objective of the project (use the project charter as a communication tool).

▶ Make sure each potential team member knows the importance of the project and how it fulfills a vital ministry for the church and to God.

▶ Ensure that each potential team member feels valued as part of the team, affirming that each one's skills are critical to achieving this important work of the church.

► Provide clear details on the role you want the person to play on the team (use the Role and Responsibility Matrix [fig. 5A] as a communication tool).

► Provide insight into your vision for the full team (number of team members, who else might be on the team, time commitment, meeting plans, etc.).

► Ask each person, "If you were to serve on this team, what would be your motivation? What would make you feel good about participating?"

► Make sure each person is clear and accepting of the concept of working together as a team.

Once the team members are in place, add names beside each "role and responsibility" line item on the Role and Responsibility Matrix (fig. 5B).

Team Meeting

Next, schedule a project kickoff meeting with the full team so that everyone can start to get to know one another, review the objective, understand each person's role and responsibility, and solicit ideas about the schedule for subsequent meetings. Discuss the vision for working together jointly, as project team and project manager, to document the project plan and schedule to achieve the project tasks and objectives.

In this initial meeting, it is important for the team to get to know each other. Ice breakers and group exercises that help build knowledge of team members are a big help. Having food or snacks often helps to make this meeting fun and supports team building. Additionally, during this meeting, the team will want to do the following:

► Refine and agree on the previously set objectives.

► Refine and agree on the target completion or implementation date.

FIGURE 5B

Role and Responsibility Matrix

Project Name: Children's Shelter Dinner   **Target Date:** 8/17/17
Document Revision Date: May 5, 2017   **Project Manager:** Jane Doe

Role	Responsibility	Name
Project Champion	• Provide advice to project manager. • Give advice on suggested team members. • Assist with conflict resolution.	Pastor James
Advisory Board (Board of Deacons)	• Provide high-level input. • Approve budget. • Prayer/look for discipleship opportunities	Administrative Board Members (see church officer list)
Project Manager	• Manage project activities. • Lead team to achieve objectives, schedule, and budget. • Coordinate selection of team members.	Camryn Lee
Menu Planning and Food Preparation	• Recommend menu. • Coordinate food preparation plan. • Determine plan for cooks.	Kelly Herbert
Servers/Greeters	• Determine service plan—buffet style or serve at tables. • Refill drinks.	Joe Santos
Dining Hall Setup and Cleanup	• Set up tables and chairs. • Place tablecloths. • Be prepared to clean spills. • Clean up dining hall after event.	Asia Chen

▶ Review and understand the budget.

▶ Understand the project scope.

One final note: The team you have just formed is the core team. Once the full team works through documenting the project plan, additional team member needs may be identified.

Planning Fundamentals

When you are at the planning phase, your congregation, pastor or leader, and administrative board have given you the initial go-ahead for the project. As a starting point, you have a general understanding of the objective, outcomes, and budget. Now you need a full plan of execution—who does what, when, and how.

Let's begin with a basic understanding of the idea of project planning. Project planning, be it for a church or a secular organization, is the phase of project management that involves preparation of schedules, such as a Gantt diagram (fig. 5H), on how project activities will be sequenced and timed, and who does the various tasks. Even if you don't use a Gantt chart, project planning still can be done in a simplified format with a task list detailing who will do what, along with starting and finishing times. It is in the planning phase that the church project team works to clarify the answers to the questions, "who, what, when, why, how much, and how long?"[9]

In church project planning, with the direction of the Holy Spirit, the church is seeking to understand fully the scope of the project it is addressing (e.g., will we conduct 2017 vacation Bible school for children ages six to sixteen only, or for children, teens, and adults?) and to define the appropriate process for completing the project (e.g., what is the best way for the church to implement a project to renovate the basement bathrooms?). A documented plan will also include the duration for each of the various tasks (e.g., length of time required to obtain supplies). A task is any activity that needs to be completed within a defined time period to achieve the project goal or objective goals. As necessary, work tasks are grouped for efficiency and commonality for who is doing the work. An additional consideration is to look at the dependencies between tasks. In other words, are there specific tasks that cannot be completed until other tasks are done first?

By defining the tasks required, along with grouping tasks as necessary and understanding dependencies, you now have a foundation for determining how many additional team members and with what skills are required. Further assessment of the time commitments needed from each volunteer for the project (sometimes referred to as "workload") will allow you to prepare a more refined project estimate and schedule.

Your next step is to schedule a meeting where project team members and the project manager work together to prepare the plan. Many project management professionals highlight five steps in preparing your project plan.[10] Here are the steps as I have implemented them in my own project planning experience:

1. Define what must be done.

2. Sequence the work.

3. Estimate resources for what must be done.

4. Estimate activity durations.

5. Develop a schedule.

Define What Must Be Done

Using the project objective (refer to your project charter), list the key tasks that must be done. Don't worry about sequence yet; this will be done during project scheduling. Figure 5C provides an example for a project where the trustee board is planning to renovate a restroom in the church.

In this example, the four key tasks are cleaning, removing tiles, painting walls, and installing new tiles. Once these have been identified, the team needs to define subtasks for each key task. Again, the main idea is to capture all tasks that must be completed (see fig. 5D).

Break each main task down into subtasks so you have a clear understanding of what must be done. However, don't try to make this too detailed. Ultimately you will need to assign someone to do each task, so the details need to address only the work that will be assigned.

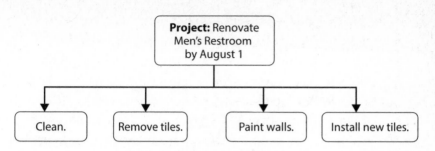

FIGURE 5C
Work Breakdown Plan

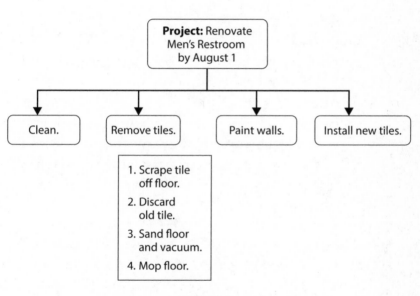

FIGURE 5D
Project Tasks with Subtasks

Now that you have an understanding of the tasks and subtasks required, list each using a template similar to figure 5E. This will be the format used for preparing your final project schedule. At this point, concentrate on capturing all tasks. (We will focus on the details of your full project schedule in the next section.) The template in figure 5E was created using Microsoft Excel. You can also create a table in any word processing package or draw a table by hand. By searching the Internet, you can find various sophisticated programs that will help you prepare a project plan and schedule—some at a cost, such as Microsoft Project, and others that are free, such as Asana, which is one of the most popular project management software applications.

FIGURE 5E
Project Task Listing

TASK	Resource	Start Date	Finish Date	1	2	3
Cleaning						
Mop / disinfect floors						
Mop / disinfect particians						
Mop / disinfect doors						
Remove all supplies / items on floors and walls						
Clean sinks, mirrors, etc., and mask for painting						
Remove tiles						
Scrape floor tiles from floor						
Discard old tiles						
Sand floor / vacuum						
Mop floor						
Paint Walls						
Install new tiles						

In the example shown, you will see the listing of the tasks and subtasks from the example shown in figure 5D.

Sequence the Work

At this point, you have listed all the tasks required to achieve the objective of the project and the required deliverables. The next step is to put the tasks in sequence. For example, if your project is to put on vacation Bible school, and the task listing includes sending communication to the local newspaper, you will need to set the location, dates, time, and registration deadlines, as well as develop the theme, prior to writing a press release and sending it to the newspaper.

Church: First Baptist Church **Document Revision Date:** October 13, 2016
Project Name: Men's Bathroom Renovation **Project Manager:** _____
Document Issue Date: October 1, 2016

November																										
4	5	6	7	8	9	10	11	12	13	14	15	16	17	18	19	20	21	22	23	24	25	26	27	28	29	30

In considering our example in figure 5E, we have five subtasks under "Cleaning." The first subtask is to clean the floors. But once the tasks of removing tiles and masking things such as sinks are done, the likelihood of the floor being dirty again and needing a recleaning is high. Thus the effectiveness of one step becomes dependent on another. For planning purposes, the project team likely needs to resequence these subtasks.

Your goal is to make sure the work is planned correctly and done efficiently. So during this sequencing phase of planning, the project manager and project team will need to look at the task list and identify any dependencies of related tasks and document them appropriately in the project schedule. For example, will the task of removing floor tiles have an impact on the task of painting? The sequencing of the work will determine when your human resources can start their part of the work.

Here is a case in point. Let's say that for the church restroom renovation example, the human resource for retiling the floor is available only on Thursday because she is going on a family vacation starting Friday. With this constraint, any task that needs to be done prior to Thursday becomes a dependency. If it is not completed by then, your schedule will slip until after the tile resource returns from vacation. That may be after your due date for completing the project. (For instance, if this renovation is for the parsonage, and a new pastor is due to move in on Monday, not getting the tile completed by Thursday is a problem.)

As your project team reviews each task required to meet your schedule, be sure to give critical thinking to the different tasks' dependencies and relationships; they can impact your task start and finish dates.

Estimate Resources for What Must Be Done

Susan is an energetic Christian, eager to reach out and serve her church community. Her day job as an accountant in a large tech firm has allowed her to hear about this concept of project management. At this point, there are no projects in accounting, and most of her work focuses on cost controls. But Susan has always wondered if project management can be used in the church. Her church, a medium-sized congregation in an urban setting, does many events, but the term *project* never gets used. The church and its pastor have been talking about what they can do to reach out into the community so they can get to know the community better and so that the community can get to know them.

One evening over coffee with some church members, an idea came to Susan's mind. Suddenly, with excitement, she said to her friends, "I know what we can do to reach out to our neighborhood. We can put on a summer community festival. We can invite all of the neighbors and their kids. We can have food, games, and booths where we read with children, share the gospel, and give out Bibles for kids and adults. Our praise band can play music. It would be a great way to get face-to-face with our neighbors! It would be a perfect project for our church next summer! I would love to lead a project like that in our church!" Susan and her friends prayed about the idea and decided they all liked it and wanted to participate in such a project. They eventually discussed the idea with the pastor and the administrative board. Everyone liked the idea, and several people volunteered to help. After discussions about timing, cost, and other planning details, the board voted to put on the festival during the upcoming summer and christened Susan the "project manager."

When Susan got back to work, during her lunch hour she shared the news about her church project with one of her coworkers, Michael, who had engineering project management experience. Over the next few weeks, Michael gave Susan a tutorial on project management, along with some advice based on his experience. One point Michael highlighted was this: "A project succeeds because of its people, their ability to work together, and your ability to lead them. Finding committed people who want to be part of the project is key. The same would be true in the church."

Because project teams in the church are made up of volunteers, they generally work on the project part-time, after or along with their commitments to their families, jobs, community, and church positions. Therefore, as a project management team, you must estimate the time required for each task. This preliminary estimate can be used for planning time and for developing a cost estimate for the church. It is critical also for your communication with individuals as you request them to volunteer. To help volunteers understand what you are expecting them to commit to, you must have a clearly defined scope of the work. You may be able to estimate time requirements for some tasks, but if you are not an expert in some area, allow the potential project team member to use his or her knowledge of the task to form an estimate, or ask someone else with knowledge to weigh in so that you can make a good decision on time commitment.

In his book *Project Management*, Gary Heerkens, project management professional and consultant, suggests asking the questions below when seeking resources to work on your team. I have followed each of his suggestions with my perspective from a church context:[11]

1. Does the candidate have the knowledge and skills to do the job? Technical and functional skills? Problem-solving skills? Interpersonal skills?

    Church project consideration: Knowledge and skills to do the job are key. Even though the project is done in a volunteer setting, don't overlook the importance of getting the right person (not just a warm body) with the right knowledge and people skills.

2. Does the candidate have the desired personal characteristics for the job?

    Church project consideration: Even in the church, there are members who prefer to do things their way only. The ability to work as a team and listen and empathize with others is critical on a church project.

3. Does the candidate believe in the goals of the project and seem likely to enthusiastically support it?

    Church project consideration: When you have team members on your church project who have passion for the ministry, you have an added asset when things get off schedule and you need a new option. These will be the people who say, "We can do all things through Christ, who strengthens us" (see Philippians 4:13).

4. Does the candidate have the time to be able to devote to the project?

    Church project consideration: Certain people in your church will have the perfect skill set for your project. But if they really can't commit the time due to other responsibilities, whether in the church or in family life, don't settle. Settling and hoping their time works out risks your project success. Keep looking for someone with passion for the project and available time.

5. Is the candidate compatible with other team members either already identified or under consideration?

    Church project consideration: Even in the church, there are members who work best in an individual contributor role as opposed to a team environment. There are people in the church who are difficult to work with also. Keep this in mind, even if they have the skills needed for the project.

Project Task Listing with Resources

TASK	Resource	Start Date	Finish Date	1	2	3
Cleaning						
Mop / disinfect floors	John Smith					
Mop / disinfect particians	John Smith					
Mop / disinfect doors	John Smith					
Remove all supplies / items on floors and walls	John Smith					
Clean sinks, mirrors, etc., and mask for painting	John Smith					
Remove tiles						
Scrape floor tiles from floor	Jane Doe					
Discard old tiles	Jane Doe					
Sand floor / vacuum	Jane Doe					
Mop floor	Jane Doe					
Paint Walls	Carol Painter					
Install new tiles						

6. Does the candidate regard participation on your project as an important function or rather as an intrusion on his or her "real job"?

Church project consideration: Even though Scripture teaches us "whatever you do, whether in word or deed, do it all in the name of the Lord Jesus" (Colossians 3:17, NIV), our humanness directs our thinking toward "what's in it for me?" Thus the church project manager needs to be sensitive to making sure that project volunteers feel they are making an important contribution to the church project and to the kingdom of God.

In summary, this step is where the project manager, with the help of other church leadership, determines what resources

November																										
4	5	6	7	8	9	10	11	12	13	14	15	16	17	18	19	20	21	22	23	24	25	26	27	28	29	30

are needed to pull off the project. Included is the identification of resources in the church as well as in the community. Remember that most church project team members will not be 100 percent available to your project, as they will also be juggling other life responsibilities. (The same likely applies to the project manager.) Lastly, in this step, you will assign resources to each of the tasks shown on your project schedule template. I recommend, as best as possible, breaking down the tasks so you can assign one task to one resource to avoid assigning multiple tasks to a given resource. This may create a larger project schedule for a complex project, but it allows the project manager better control in allocating and tracking resources during the project execution phase. Figure 5F gives an example.

Estimate Activity Durations

Now that you have tasks defined, a team in place, and other resources (budget, space, supplies, etc.) assigned, the next step is to estimate the *time required* and *duration* of each task. From a church project management perspective, let me define the two terms. *Time* refers to how many hours it will take to accomplish a particular task. *Duration* describes the number of calendar periods (days, weeks) it takes from the time the execution of an element starts to the time the task is completed. Duration should not be confused with actual working hours; rather, it is a way to plan for how certain elements of a task can be completed when not in immediate sequential order.

For example, take a project requiring painting. The task of painting requires eight hours, which should include time for getting supplies (two hours), applying a primer coat (two hours), and then completing the final color coat with cleanup (four hours). So, for estimating purposes, the work for that task will be eight hours, which suggests one work day. However, the schedule is set up across three days because getting supplies is done on November 11, the primer coat is done on November 12, and the final painting and cleanup are done on November 13. Therefore, the task's duration is three days.

In your planning process, duration should not be confused with working hours, but neither should the time estimated for actual labor be viewed as transpiring in rapid-fire sequence. In the example above, primer needs time to dry before a final coat can be applied! In other projects, you may need to plan for a two-week administrative wait for the thirty-minute task of filing for a license or zoning permit before getting started. Such gaps in duration may allow for creative use of limited human resources, however. The same volunteer who filed the paperwork for one task might be willing to purchase painting supplies (or apply a primer coat) for another task in the interim period.

I mentioned earlier that those involved in the church project should be involved in the planning process, including estimation of task time and duration. This point bears reviewing since project management research suggests such inclusion of those involved in the implementation avoids a common pitfall of planning and underpins team support of the church project endeavor. Heerkens suggests:

> The people who will be working on your project should be heavily involved in planning their portion of it. There are at least two good reasons for this. First, the planning outputs will undoubtedly be more accurate as the task performers are probably more knowledgeable than you—after all, it's what they do. Second, involving them during the planning stage is likely to make them significantly more willing to participate and more committed to succeeding. People often feel compelled to live up to what they've promised.[12]

Now that you have involved the full team in preparing the estimates, the details need to be captured in a single location—your project plan template. Once complete, the template will look similar to figure 5G, as shown on the following pages.

Develop a Schedule

This next step, where you document the project schedule, is one of the most critical parts of project planning. What *is* the project schedule? Although there are varied definitions, this is one I like best:

> The project schedule is the tool that communicates what work needs to be performed, which resources of the organization will perform the work and the time frames in which that work needs to be performed. The project schedule should reflect all of the work associated with delivering the project on time. Without a full and complete schedule, the project manager will be unable to communicate the complete effort, in terms of cost and resources, necessary to deliver the project.[13]

FIGURE 5G

Project Plan Template with Resources and Time Estimates

TASK	Resource	Start Date	Finish Date	1	2	3
Cleaning						
Mop / disinfect floors	John Smith	Nov. 1	Nov. 5			
Mop / disinfect particians	John Smith	Nov. 1	Nov. 1			
Mop / disinfect doors	John Smith	Nov. 2	Nov. 3			
Remove all supplies / items on floors and walls	John Smith	Nov. 4	Nov. 4			
Clean sinks, mirrors, etc., and mask for painting	John Smith	Nov. 5	Nov. 5			
Remove tiles						
Scrape floor tiles from floor	Jane Doe	Nov. 6	Nov. 6			
Discard old tiles	Jane Doe	Nov. 7	Nov. 7			
Sand floor / vacuum	Jane Doe	Nov. 8	Nov. 8			
Mop floor	Jane Doe	Nov. 9	Nov. 9			
Paint Walls	Carol Painter	Nov. 11	Nov. 13			
Install new tiles						

Project scheduling is an integral part of the project planning process in that the schedule establishes the timelines, delivery requirements, and availability of project resources, whether they be people, learning materials, equipment, or supplies. For this reason, any church project without a documented, detailed schedule is a church project destined to have issues down the road.

A well-managed project requires a proper schedule to ensure success. The project schedule will help to organize all tasks related to a project in a detailed, graphic form, making it easier

Church: First Baptist Church
Project Name: Men's Bathroom Renovation
Document Issue Date: October 1, 2016

Document Revision Date: October 13, 2016
Project Manager: _____ Asia Kaate _____

November																										
4	5	6	7	8	9	10	11	12	13	14	15	16	17	18	19	20	21	22	23	24	25	26	27	28	29	30

to manage the project process. Project managers can more easily see and manage tasks, progress, and associated resources assignments when using a project schedule.

Furthermore, the project schedule is a living document. In this step, you will create the first revision of the schedule. As your project progresses and as the team meets on a regular basis, you will update the schedule based on input from the project team and in response to actual project progress. For example, a new task may be added to the project schedule. With this change, you will want to change the schedule to "Revision 2" or use a revision date, such as "revised October 15, 2017." So, even though you prepare your schedule at this point in the planning process, it is never a static document. You will revise it based on team updates, adding notes about task completion (in percentages) and in response to project manager feedback. Without maintaining a well-documented and up-to-date schedule, you will never know when you are going to finish your project.

Many church projects get started from the idea phase, overlooking the need for and benefits of preparing a proper schedule. As work progresses, meeting notes get translated into minutes for distribution to the team. Yet when questions arise about whether the project is on schedule, subjective guesses, not project dates, are used to formulate an answer. But a clear and accurate assessment of project status is important, not only for the project manager but also for key administrative leaders and pastors who have championed and authorized the project. They will want to know status and rate of progression. Without a proper project schedule, assessing your progress is difficult.

A church project manager should be able to give the progression of the project in percentages—whether the project is 64 percent complete or 10 percent. Without a regularly updated project schedule, it is very likely that the project manager, as well as team members, may have to spend extra time trying to figure out where tasks are and what problems need to be solved, trying to make sure the project can be completed on time. And at the end of the process, the quality of the finished project might be poor, the volunteer experience of your team might be negative, and they won't be likely to volunteer again.

A good project schedule should consist of a written plan, with firm dates, clearly identified resource needs, and specific assignments for who is doing what and when. If you have done the previous steps with intentionality and integrity, this phase should be facilitated with relative ease because you already have most of the information you need. In summary, in this phase your objective is to document the following:

- ▶ What must be done?
- ▶ Who will do it?
- ▶ How will it be done?
- ▶ When must it be done?
- ▶ How much will it cost?
- ▶ What do we need to do it?

Recapping the work you have done so far, you now have input and estimates from your project team for their parts of the projects. As you look to synchronize all of this information, your goal as project manager and team is to analyze the project schedule inputs and examine the sequences and inevitable scheduling constraints. Thus the goal of this step is to validate all project schedule inputs—the time and duration estimates, as well as resource allocations, to ensure that they correctly model the planned work. You will also want to make sure that the members of the project team are not overloaded or underloaded (often referred to as "resource leveling" in the project management field) so that project dates are realistic and the resources are appropriately assigned.

The Project Management Institute, the world's leading not-for-profit professional membership association for the project management profession, which does global advocacy, collaboration, education, and research, emphasizes that "by creating a solid schedule at the start of the project, project managers can help curb cost overruns, resource shortages or excessive change requests."[14] To further make this point, a panel of project scheduling professionals has offered six tips for creating a solid church project schedule.[15]

1. Realize the importance of the schedule.

Project managers and the project management team often do not put enough emphasis on the schedule. However, a good church project schedule should touch on standard project management knowledge areas, such as management of the following:

- ▶ scope (i.e., keeping the big picture in view)
- ▶ time
- ▶ cost
- ▶ quality (of the process, of relationships, of the desired outcomes)
- ▶ human resources (volunteers, vendors, community partners)
- ▶ communications
- ▶ risk
- ▶ procurement
- ▶ stakeholders (champions, the congregation, volunteers, donors)[16]

Consider the following scenario. You are leading a project in which the church is replacing part of the sidewalk near the church education building. The task of pouring the concrete is to take place in late fall, before the weather turns too cold. If the task is not completed before the first freeze, there is a risk that the project will have to be put off until the following spring. Thus the project manager will list this item as a risk because weather conditions might cause a slip in the schedule. If a delay does occur, this schedule change will affect other areas of the project and will have an impact on tasks to be completed later. The schedule therefore becomes the central focus and the foundational tool for managing the project.

2. Identify the availability of team members.

A resource inventory is needed to plan the whole project and to decide which path you will take to execute the project. Who will be available to work on the project? Are there any holes, or will any team member be stretched too thin? This is especially important in environments where budgets are tight and many organizations hesitate to take on more staff members. Once the project team has been established, ask for their input on the schedule to ensure that it is reasonable.

3. Build the schedule around desired outcomes.

Wanting to build a schedule around tasks is human nature, but that method can cause problems. The flaw with that task-focused approach is that a scheduler cannot easily tell if a requested change by organizational leadership, for example, is actually within the project scope. Project schedulers should build the schedule around what you are trying to achieve.

4. Include regular milestones.

Establish milestones within the schedule and check those milestones frequently. That way, if a project is expected to last for eight months, you do not want to get to month four and realize you are already seriously behind schedule. If you miss milestones that occur in the first couple of months of the project, you will be better equipped to communicate a new expected date of completion—or to adjust subsequent deadlines to get the project back on schedule.

5. Expect that the schedule will change.

Remember that I said earlier that the project schedule is not a static document. This is because project tasks and church stakeholders' needs sometimes change. The project schedule is really an assumption about what might happen and when. It is your job to continue to understand the reason for any variances and make appropriate changes to the schedule to meet the changing project landscape. This would include a contingency plan. For example, if the desired painting supplies are backordered, then the dates for your three-day-duration painting task will need to be adjusted. Or perhaps a different human resource might be identified to secure the supplies from a different vendor who still has inventory. As a contingency plan, you might go back to the committee that chose the desired paint color or finish and ask for a runner-up paint option if their first choice is discontinued or delayed for too long.

6. Have a process for managing change.

Church project managers must be willing to shift gears to help a project stay on track. Keep track of changes and develop a rubric to assess what type or degree of change is deemed significant enough to warrant alternate action (referred to by project management experts as the "change-control process"). For example, if there is added cost, you may need to get approval for additional spending.

I recommend preparing your schedule in a group session with the full team. Try to set aside a block of time—at least two hours—when everyone can meet together, share their input, ask questions, and prepare the final draft with everyone on the same page. During this session, use a computer with a projector or display monitor or at least a newsprint flip chart so that everyone can see what will make up the final product.

The contents of the project plan and schedule are as follows:

- ▶ Listing of each task
  - In sequence
  - Identify tasks with critical timing, differentiated from those with some flexibility (sometimes called "float" by project managers; e.g., purchasing supplies has some

float, but painting must be timed for completion before church anniversary)

► Listing of milestones

► Assigning of resources for all tasks and milestones (i.e., who will do each task)

► Setting of start and finish dates for each task

► Preparing of graphic to show task timing and task linkages

Figure 5H provides an example of a project schedule. Most project management literature will display an example of a project schedule using this format, often referred to as a Gantt chart. Depending on the complexity of your project, a simpler schedule is acceptable. Figure 5I provides an example of a simplified project schedule.

Once the project manager and project team have completed the schedule, it is time to review the schedule with church leadership, including the pastor, for initial feedback. After securing that important feedback, make necessary changes. You will want to establish a baseline project schedule document before you move to schedule execution. In other words, this is your starting version of the schedule with the date of the schedule for this first draft. This will ensure that the original dates are saved, and the project manager and team can compare schedule changes once the execution phase has started.

One final thought. Throughout this chapter, I have made reference to various figures and templates used in the church project management process. As you plan your project, it is a good idea for the project manager and team to complete prepare their templates and store them in a formal project notebook or electronic file share, i.e., Dropbox, Microsoft OneDrive, Apple iCloud, where so that the team has ready access and so that there is an archive of project documents that can be used and referenced for future projects.

Church Project Schedule (GANTT Chart)

Task	Resource	Start Date	Finish Date	August			
				wk. 1	wk. 2	wk. 3	wk. 4
Project kickoff	Team	Aug. 3	Aug. 3	�			
Review plan with worship committee	James	Aug. 10	Aug. 14		▓		
Revise plan with input from worship committee	Edward	Aug. 17	Aug. 21			▓	
Final review with leadership staff	Ellen	Aug. 24	Aug. 28				▓
Communicate plan to congregation	James	Aug. 31	Sept. 4				
Identify potential paint contractors	Authur / Sharon	Sept. 7	Sept. 11				
Review scope and planned timing with contractors; request quote	Robert	Sept. 14	Sept. 25				
Contractors review facility	Contractors / Robert	Sept. 28	Oct. 2				
Receive quotes	Michael	Oct. 5	Oct. 16				
Quote review sessions	Team	Oct. 19	Oct. 23				
Get answers to questions about quotes	Michael	Oct. 26	Oct. 30				
Select contractor	Team	Nov. 2	Nov. 6				
Review selection with leadership staff; clarify quotations	James	Nov. 9	Nov. 13				
Award contract to selected paint contractor	James	Nov. 19	Nov. 23				
Paint sanctuary	Contract Awardee	Jan. 4	Jan. 15				
Paint bathrooms	Contract Awardee	Jan. 18	Jan. 22				
Paint basement / classrooms	Contract Awardee	Jan. 25	Feb. 5				
Paint touch ups	Contract Awardee	Feb. 8	Feb. 12				
Wrap up punch list with contractors; quality check	Awardee / Team	Feb. 15	Feb. 18				
Project review and evaluation	Team	Feb. 19	Feb. 19				
Project team celebration	Team	Feb. 24	Feb. 24				
Project closure	Team	Feb. 26	Feb. 26				

Church: Broadway Community Church
Project Name: Church Painting
Document Issue Date: June 13, 2016

Document Revision Date: July 13, 2016
Project Manager: E.W. Dade

September				October				November				December				January				February			
wk. 1	wk. 2	wk. 3	wk. 4	wk. 1	wk. 2	wk. 3	wk. 4	wk. 1	wk. 2	wk. 3	wk. 4	wk. 1	wk. 2	wk. 3	wk. 4	wk. 1	wk. 2	wk. 3	wk. 4	wk. 1	wk. 2	wk. 3	wk. 4

Church Project Schedule (Simple)

Church: Broadway Community Church
Project Name: Church Painting
Document Issue Date: June 13, 2016

Document Revision Date: July 13, 2016
Project Manager: E.W. Dade

Task	Resource	Start Date	Finish Date
Project kickoff	Team	Aug. 3	Aug. 3
Review plan with worship committee	James	Aug. 10	Aug. 14
Revise plan with input from worship committee	Edward	Aug. 17	Aug. 21
Final review with leadership staff	Ellen	Aug. 24	Aug. 28
Communicate plan to congregation	James	Aug. 31	Sept. 4
Identify potential paint contractors	Authur / Sharon	Sept. 7	Sept. 11
Review scope and planned timing with contractors; request quote	Robert	Sept. 14	Sept. 25
Contractors review facility	Contractors / Robert	Sept. 28	Oct. 2
Receive quotes	Michael	Oct. 5	Oct. 16
Quote review sessions	Team	Oct. 19	Oct. 23
Get answers to questions about quotes	Michael	Oct. 26	Oct. 30
Select contractor	Team	Nov. 2	Nov. 6
Review selection with leadership staff; clarify quotations	James	Nov. 9	Nov. 13
Award contract to selected paint contractor	James	Nov. 19	Nov. 23
Paint sanctuary	Contract Awardee	Jan. 4	Jan. 15
Paint bathrooms	Contract Awardee	Jan. 18	Jan. 22
Paint basement / classrooms	Contract Awardee	Jan. 25	Feb. 5
Paint touch ups	Contract Awardee	Feb. 8	Feb. 12
Wrap up punch list with contractors; quality check	Awardee / Team	Feb. 15	Feb. 18
Project review and evaluation	Team	Feb. 19	Feb. 19
Project team celebration	Team	Feb. 24	Feb. 24
Project closure	Team	Feb. 26	Feb. 26

NOTES

1. T. Carlos, "Reasons Why Projects Fail," Project Smart, accessed November 30, 2016, www.projectsmart.co.uk/reasons-why-projects-fail.php.

2. J. P. Lewis, *Fundamentals of Project Management* (New York: AMACOM, 2007), 24.

3. S. Madsen, "Collaborative Planning—7 Steps to Creating a Project Plan with Your Team," *PM Perspectives* blog, February 12, 2015, www.esi-intl.co.uk/blogs/pmoperspectives/index.php/collaborative-planning-7-steps-creating-project-plan-team/.

4. R. Velarde, "What Is the Church?" Focus on the Family, 2009, www.focusonthefamily.com/faith/the-study-of-god/why-study-god/what-is-the-church.

5. Gideons International is an association of Christian professionals and businessmen and their wives dedicated to telling people about Jesus through sharing personally and by providing Bibles and New Testaments.

6. S. J. Ellis, "Why Volunteer?" Energize Inc., accessed November 30, 2016, www.energizeinc.com/art/why-volunteer.

7. T. Wolfe, *Managing a Nonprofit Organization in the Twenty-First Century* (New York: Simon and Schuster, 1999), 99.

8. Ibid.

9. Lewis, *Fundamentals of Project Management*, 24.

10. A. Makar, "How to Build a Project Schedule in 5 Easy Steps," Project Smart, August 25, 2010, www.projectsmart.co.uk/how-to-build-a-project-schedule-in-5-easy-steps.php.

11. G. R. Heerkens, *Project Management* (New York: McGraw-Hill, 2002), 82.

12. Ibid., 104.

13. "Project Scheduling," Project Insight, accessed November 30, 2016, www.projectinsight.net/project-management-basics/project-management-schedule.

14. A. Aramburu, M. Colodzin, J. Lukas, P. Weaver, "Seven Tips on How to Build a Solid Schedule," PMPPassport, March 2009,

www.pmi.org/passport/mar09/passport_mar09_seven-tips-on-how-
to-build-a-solid-schedule.html.

15. Ibid.

16. *A Guide to the Project Management Body of Knowledge
(PMBOK® Guide)*, Knowledge Area and Process Groups (Newtown
Square, PA: Project Management Institute, 2013).

➤

CHAPTER 6

Executing Your Church Project and Controlling the Schedule

Implementation, doing the work you have planned, is the next step in church project management. The standard project management term for this is *project execution*. During this phase, the project team and the project manager work to achieve each task on schedule.

Jason Westland, a leading expert in project management, points out the following in his seminal text, *The Project Management Life Cycle*:

> The execution phase is typically the longest phase of the project in terms of duration. It is the phase within which the deliverables are physically constructed and presented to the customer for acceptance. To ensure that the [church] requirements are met, the project manager monitors and controls the activities, resources and expenditures required to build [or achieve] each deliverable. A number of management processes are undertaken to ensure that the project proceeds as planned.[1]

Bottom line, all the project plans and schedules you and your team prepare are worth nothing without a good project execution effort. This phase is necessary to make sure church project deliverables and objectives will meet church and ministry expectations.

So the question we must now address is, "How do we do this phase of the project?" This phase has four components:

▶ Project team communication

▶ Project team work

▶ Monitor and control

▶ Organization communication

Project Team Communication

A critical step at the start of any project is to make sure that all project team members are in alignment. The bedrock of this alignment is communication. Recent studies have demonstrated that "among those organizations considered highly effective communicators, 80 percent of projects meet original goals, versus only 52 percent at their minimally effective counterparts" and that "highly effective communicators are also more likely to deliver projects on time—71 percent versus 37 percent—and within budget—76 percent versus 48 percent."[2]

In thinking of church project management, consider the following three types of communication.

Leadership Communication

▶ **Communicate with God.** Never forget that church projects are done for the glory of God and to serve God's people. Therefore regular prayer is mandatory as the project team continually seeks the Spirit's guidance in executing the work. This can and should happen corporately, in team meetings and working groups, as well as individually by the project leader and team members in their personal times of devotion and Bible study.

▶ **Communicate with the pastor.** Specifically, highlight the project's impact on the church or issues that have an impact on project success.

▶ **Communicate with church leaders.** This communication may take place via standing meetings, email correspondence, conference calls, or video conferencing. The main thing is to establish the regular communication channel based on what works best for the leaders involved.

Stakeholder Communication

▶ Stakeholders may include members of the congregation, community partners, supporters and donors, vendors, and neighbors affected by the ministry project.

▶ Tools for communication with stakeholders outside of the congregation include an email list, press releases, free or paid media publicity, neighborhood forums, one-on-one meetings, and intentional networking with community support agencies.

▶ Internal communication tools include phone calls, emails, updates on the church website and social media pages, status reports at congregational meetings, and updates in the church bulletin, newsletter, or from the pulpit on Sunday morning.

Internal Team Communication

▶ Communicate internally among project manager and project team members.

▶ Such communications will involve highlighting upcoming task deadlines, potential issues, schedule adjustments, and appropriate action planning, as well as general team communication about meeting dates and task assignments.

► Agree from the outset on the formal and informal modes for team communication so that all team members are clear on how to get and share information.

► Team communication may happen using numerous methods, from face-to-face discussions to email correspondence and phone conferences. Establish a regular (standing) project review meeting with a meeting agenda drafted and circulated in advance. At these meetings, review the project schedule, project issues, and any information shared through other less formal or inclusive team communications.

All team members must be clear about their roles and responsibilities, the importance of their work, the full schedule as well as the schedule for their own parts of the project, and the team communication strategy. Establish to whom and using what method individual team members should communicate issues when they arise. For example, do team members call the project manager or wait until the next project meeting? Figure 6A illustrates the interconnection of the three components of project communication.

As a church project manager, you must understand that communication for the project is a deliverable for which you are personally responsible. Communication has a large influence over your project's success or failure. Oftentimes lack of communication or missteps in communication result in misunderstandings, misinformation, and disgruntled volunteer project team members. The impact of poor communication in a volunteer setting should not be underestimated since volunteers are already burdened by normal daily responsibilities of work and family. With the limited and valuable time they

FIGURE 6A

Project Communication Interconnection

volunteer to be part of the project, ineffective project meetings and related communication issues can become a source of frustration for them.

Conversely, being viewed as a good communicator goes a long way toward building strong team dynamics, as well as your own reputation as a good leader. This is critical to project success. One of my volunteer experiences associated with project management brought me into contact with Tom McKee and his son Jonathan, authors of the book *The New Breed: Understanding and Equipping the 21st Century Volunteer*.[3] Tom did some research on why people quit volunteer experiences. One hypothesis was that people's plates are too full with other life responsibilities. Tom questioned whether that was really true and found something quite different.

In his article "People Don't Quit Volunteering because They Are Too Busy: They Quit because . . . The Top Seven Reasons

Volunteers Quit," Tom uncovers four of the seven reasons that are related to communication:

1. Too much wasted time in useless or unproductive meetings

2. Lack of communication

3. Lack of professionalism

4. The volunteer leader who doesn't know how to lead[4]

The bottom line is that the church project manager must, backed by prayer, ensure good communication with the project team, with stakeholders (such as the congregation and the community), and with church leadership.

Project Team Work

The bulk of the work of a church project gets done by a project team, so solid teamwork is of utmost importance. None of us is strong in every area necessary to complete a project, and that is why the Holy Spirit equips the church with a variety of gifts (Ephesians 4:11-13). We all come together with different gifts and abilities that can be used for the work of ministry. Moreover, many in the church have gifts that they have developed and applied successfully in their careers yet have not considered applying these gifts in the context of the church. Projects provide an excellent opportunity to apply the varied gifts and talents that we have been blessed with. And since we are many parts, each part is important to having an effective whole. This is a good thing. How many times have we heard a church member complain that most of the work gets done by only a "faithful few"? Everyone can contribute, and our churches need every member involved in ministry.

Paul reminds us in Romans 12 that bodies, including church bodies (think congregation or church project teams) don't function well unless they work together. Church project teams need to work as a body to function well (see 1 Corinthians 12:12-27).

How is this done? Let's look at some Scripture passages that emphasize teamwork:

▶ **Ecclesiastes 4:9-12.** "It's better to have a partner than go it alone. Share the work, share the wealth. And if one falls down, the other helps, But if there's no one to help, tough! Two in a bed warm each other. Alone, you shiver all night. By yourself you're unprotected. With a friend you can face the worst. Can you round up a third? A three-stranded rope isn't easily snapped" (MSG). The lesson in a nutshell? A team can accomplish more than an individual.

▶ **Nehemiah 4.** Read this whole chapter. It is a good example of a project being done by the Lord's people. Pastor Rick Warren summarizes the work of this Scripture-based ministry project: "When the Israelites were rebuilding the wall in Jerusalem, the work got tough and they got discouraged. Finally, they just gave up. So Nehemiah reorganized the work into teams. Half would stand guard with their spears and swords and protect everyone. The other half would work. Then they'd alternate their positions. He posted everyone by groups and families so they could encourage and support each other."[5]

▶ **Mark 6:7.** In this gospel text, we discover that when Jesus sent people out in ministry, he did not send them to do the work alone. "Jesus called the Twelve to him, and sent them out in pairs. He gave them authority and power to [minister]" (MSG). He sent them out in groups of two and expected them to minister and work together.

▶ **Acts 6.** Again, read the full chapter to get another example of a team of people appointed to do the work of ministry. Specifically, seven people were chosen to serve on the ministry team to ensure the preaching and teaching of the Word and service to those in need were both done effectively.

▶ **Philippians 2:3-5, 13-14.** In Paul's letter to the church at Philippi, we observe how effective communication is important and mandated for effective ministry. "Do nothing out of selfish ambition or vain conceit. Rather, in humility value others above yourselves, not looking to your own interests but each of you to the interests of the others. In your relationships with one another, have the same mindset as Christ Jesus: . . . for it is God who works in you to will and to act in order to fulfill his good purpose. Do everything without grumbling or arguing" (NIV).

We can form guidelines from these Scriptures to use in executing church projects.

▶ **Follow the project schedule.** Everyone should work toward the schedule the team agreed on. This is a vital document to helping the team achieve its goals.

▶ **Be a team player.** Like a sports team, everyone has a position to play. All members should do their part in keeping up with the project plan (not their individual agendas) and, when needed, help other team members.

▶ **Be a self-starter.** Self-starters don't wait for the project manager to tell them to do their part. They know what they are supposed to do, and they do it. Because everyone on the team needs to be focused on the project objective, if a little something extra is needed, a self-starter does it for the good of the team.

▶ **Be a positive influence.** All teams at times have conflict that they will need to navigate. Being positive not only helps a team through these times; it can also provide a source of encouragement to team members who may be facing other life challenges.

► **Be dependable.** As technology writer Tricia Goss points out in her article "Top 10 Characteristics of an Effective Project Team," an effective project team is comprised of members who are "reliable, responsible and accountable to one another as well as to themselves . . . They adhere to that schedule because they don't want to let down their teammates—or themselves."[6]

► **Communicate often and well.** Regular communication is important. Do not wait for a meeting to communicate. Face-to-face communication after worship or a phone call before dinner are effective tools in church project management. Communicating well also means being sensitive in *how* you communicate: be a good listener, avoid offending others as you try to get your point across, and understand that in communication, what is most important is what the other person has heard, not what you said.

► **Use creativity.** As noted above, every project will at times run into snags, requiring problem solving. The benefit of the church project team is that the team encompasses a broad range of skills, gifts, and knowledge. So when a problem arises, use the knowledge you gained on the job, through community service, or in the church to solve the problem. This will help keep the project on schedule and allow the church to minister to the needs of the community and congregation based on the project plan. After all, most projects have a critical timeline that the team is working toward. If the team misses that date, you miss an important opportunity to do the work of Christ.

► **Be caring and supportive of team members.** Just as in any small group ministry, church project team members should be caring and supportive of one another, not just of the church project itself. A caring and supportive project team will pray for one another, check in with one another about personal concerns as well as project status, and inquire if teammates need help.

Monitor and Control

While executing a project, we must also monitor and control what is happening during all activities and tasks to ensure that we stay on schedule to achieve project objectives. A key component for monitor and control of the various project tasks is the project review meeting. Typically this is a weekly meeting. (If the project is large and extends over a year, such as a pastoral search project, a monthly meeting may be more appropriate.) At these meetings, the full team will be in attendance. The objective of these meetings is to have regular communication that involves everyone who is part of the project. This fosters communication with participants by reviewing the project status and comparing it to the schedule, identifying issues, and asking questions. At these meetings, team members may also discuss any proposed changes to the project plan, allowing the team to make group decisions to approve or reject proposals that contribute to timely project delivery based on planned goals and expected results.

At each project review meeting, the project manager should review the schedule, status of achieving the objective, and any concerns or communication important to the church project team. At this meeting you should be asking such questions as the following:

▶ Are we on schedule?

▶ Do we need more people?

▶ Do we need to plan for more supplies and resources?

▶ Do we need a course correction?

In addition, each person who is responsible for a critical part of the project should come prepared to discuss their status. Specifically, they will need to be prepared to share (1) their progress related to the schedule, (2) any obstacles they foresee that will hinder them from meeting their due dates, (3) actions they will take to ensure that they will stay on schedule, and (4) any help they need from the team.

To ensure an efficient meeting, here are some guidelines for conducting project meetings:

▶ **After the initial planning sessions, regular project meetings should be scheduled for no longer than one hour.** A defined time helps the project manager and team be efficient. Furthermore, since your team is made up of volunteers, be aware of their time constraints and considerate of your use of others' time. When you need more time, schedule separate sessions, phone conferences, sidebar conversations, etc., for specific people or issues on a one-on-one basis.

▶ **Always have a written agenda that can be distributed to the team prior to the meeting so they can properly prepare.** As noted in an earlier chapter, church projects are ministries that are designed to "equip the saints for the work of ministry, for building up the body of Christ" (Ephesians 4:12, ESV). So prayer and devotion should always be agenda items. Figure 6B provides a template for a meeting agenda.

▶ **Facilitate the meeting per the agenda.** Be efficient and focused. Control extraneous conversation that can take the team off topic. The project team will evaluate the project manager's leadership performance based on an effectively run project meeting. If time is not managed appropriately, the result can be frustrated team members who feel that their time is being wasted and that your leadership ability is lacking.

▶ **Allow time for questions and discussion.** Invariably, there will be questions and new items for discussion. This gives the project manager another opportunity to pick up on possible issues that might be brewing below the surface and thereby head off future problems that might arise.

▶ **Summarize key points and follow-up items at the end of the meeting.** Allow time before you close the meeting to review the important actions and decisions made by the group. This should include identification of who will do what and by when. One of the best ways to do this is to assign a team member to keep a "Project Action Item List." This list should be distributed to all team members (the next day if possible), and it should be reviewed for status of each item at the next meeting. Where possible, the goal is to complete these action items by the next meeting.

▶ **Do not micromanage.** Micromanagement is a management style in which the project manager closely observes or controls the detailed work of team members, often interjecting how tasks should be done instead of letting team members handle the implementation. In a volunteer setting, this can result in frustrated team members, who might ultimately choose to quit the team.

▶ **Adjourn at the agreed-upon time.** Conclude the meeting thanking the team for their work. Always close the meeting on an upbeat tone:
  • reiterating project accomplishments to date;
  • reinforcing team spirit by encouraging each member to watch out for one another's well-being, since people are the key foundation for project success; and
  • offering a closing prayer.

Based on the outcome of the meeting, the project manager will update the project schedule and the project action item list (fig. 6C) and distribute it to the project team in a timely manner.

FIGURE 6B
Project Review Meeting Agenda—Template

Meeting Agenda	
Project name:	Meeting date:
Attendees:	
Opening prayer/devotion/team member check-in:	
Project manager communication update	
Subtask leader #1 update	
Subtask leader #2 update	
Subtask leader #3 update	
Subtask leader #4 update	
Action item list review	
Adjourn/closing prayer (by one of the project team members)	

FIGURE 6C
Project Action Item List

Project name:		Leader:	Revision date:	
Item #	Action	Who?	When?	Status

Organizational Communication

Earlier we discussed team communication. The project manager must also consider communication in the broader context of the congregation. *Congregation* is the key word. The project you are undertaking represents the totality of the local church. So, beyond maintaining a routine communication with congregation, community, and outside church agencies (as outlined previously in this chapter) via local media, Sunday morning announcements, church newsletters, and websites, depending on the importance of the project, you may also need to provide a periodic update to church administration, deacons, or trustees of the church.

In many cases, these are the boards that approve projects, so the project manager should expect to be required to provide status reports. Although none of these leaders may be members of the project team, each is a stakeholder—"an individual, group, or organization, who may affect, be affected by, or perceive itself to be affected by a decision, activity, or outcome of a project."[7] Stakeholders are decision makers within the church, and as such, decisions or outcomes of a project may be perceived as having change impact on their scope of responsibility. As John Kotter, professor at the Harvard Business School and author of *Leading Change*, proposes, there are linkages between change management and project management, and to enable effective church organizational change (if needed), identifying and understanding how various stakeholder organizations interact with the project is key.[8]

The bottom line is this: the project manager and project team should be prepared to keep the congregation and its leadership, including the pastoral staff, updated on project progress and status. They all have a vested interest and will want to help the project team succeed. They will also be praying for the project's success. Prepare reports that are focused and provide updates on progress toward completion of your objective in relation to the project schedule. (Figure 6D provides an example of a stakeholder update status.)

Now that your project is underway, the team will continue to execute the work planned, with all team members doing their parts, as well as helping one another as needed to ensure a quality result. Hold regular project review meetings with the team throughout the duration of the project schedule. During these meetings, each team member will keep the project manager

FIGURE 6D
Project Stakeholder Update

Church: Dogwood Community Church	**Project title:** Youth Scholarships for 2017
	Project manager: Camryn Newford
Status	**Key Upcoming Activities**
On schedule to raise targeted goal of $5,000 to award scholarships by May 13, 2017	1. Holiday craft fair will be held December 3, 2016
	2. Letters to community businesses will be sent to solicit contributions mid-January 2017
Areas where project team needs help: Two volunteers needed to help with mailings in January	

and team updated on individual work and progress. After each meeting, update the schedule based on input from each team member and distribute the revised schedule to all team members. Keep the stakeholders (congregation and church leadership) in the communication loop via the project communication plan. Periodically provide verbal (at church meetings) or written updates (reports, presentations, or announcements for church media). Finally, continue to monitor the project overall and provide feedback as required to the team.

All of these activities will continue for the duration of the project until the deliverables are completed—the vacation Bible school is a success, the parsonage renovation is complete, the church history is documented and published, college scholarships are awarded to local students, the annual Community Fun Festival kicks off as planned, the annual pastor's appreciation event is held. Whether the project has a duration of three months or three years, it is vital that the church project manager and team be disciplined in execution of the project requirements, including monitoring and controlling all aspects of the project until the project is completed.

NOTES

1. J. Westland, *The Project Management Life Cycle: A Complete Step-by-Step Methodology for Initiating, Planning, Executing and Closing a Project Successfully* (Philadelphia: Kogan Page, 2007), 10.

2. "Communication: The Message Is Clear," PMI, www.pmi.org/~/media/PDF/Knowledge%20Center/Communications_whitepaper_v2.ashx, accessed November 30, 2016.

3. Tom and Jonathan McKees's book focuses on a broad range of volunteer experiences. When I was first introduced to their book, I was a volunteer leader with the Society of Manufacturing Engineers. On hearing Jonathan speak on volunteerism at one of our conferences, I shared a comment that I felt what he said also applied to the church. His response was that he too was active in a local church

and knew firsthand that it did. So I would recommend that church leaders read this book.

4. Thomas McKee, "People Don't Quit Volunteering because They Are Too Busy: They Quit because . . . The Top Seven Reasons Volunteers Quit," Volunteer Power, www.volunteerpower.com/articles/WhyPeopleQuit.asp, accessed November 30, 2016.

5. Rick Warren, "Four Bible Passages about Teamwork," Pastors.com, October 16, 2012, http://pastors.com/four-bible-passages-about-teamwork/.

6. Tricia Goss, "Top 10 Characteristics of an Effective Project Team," Bright Hub Project Management, updated January 24, 2015, www.brighthubpm.com/resource-management/72619-top-ten-characteristics-of-an-effective-project-team/#sthash.DbVcUS74.dpuf.

7. 5th Edition PMBOK® Guide—Chapter 2: Stakeholders, 4SquareViews, January 28, 2013, http://4squareviews.com/-2013/01/28/5th-edition-pmbok-guide-chapter-2-stakeholders/.

8. J. Kotter, *Leading Change*, Change Leadership Network, November 28, 2011, http://changeleadershipnetwork.org/2011/11/28/applying-kotters-change-management-principles-to-project-management/.

CHAPTER 7

→

Church Project Closure, Evaluation, and Celebration

Congratulations on completing your project! Your ministry project has achieved its objective and completed its deliverables. You and your team should be proud, and it is my prayer that the full team—project manager and project team—have learned a great deal, as well as had a spiritually fulfilling experience, knowing that your work has made an important contribution in building God's kingdom, sharing Christ's love, and planting seeds for making disciples for Christ.

At this stage, your congregation has accepted the final project deliverable. But more work is still needed. From a church project management perspective, the project is not done until you have completed the church project closure and evaluation phase.

To complete this phase, you will need to accomplish the following six requirements. Some should be done with church leadership and some with the project team, but never by the project manager in vacuum. Each of these documents should be filed in your project notebook, as mentioned at the end of chapter 5.

1. Craft a leadership feedback summary.

2. Conduct a project performance summary.

3. Clean up the project action list.

4. Convene a "lessons learned" session.

5. Complete the project notebook.

6. Organize a team celebration.

Craft a Leadership Feedback Summary

A key component of project management is to learn from each project experience so that the learning can be applied to future projects. This can be especially helpful when the project manager leads a future project or when the project team or other church members work on future projects. A good source of feedback comes from church leadership (pastor and chairpersons of the trustees, administrative board, deacons, etc.).

To document a summary of leadership feedback, the project manager should schedule a meeting with the leadership team of the church to request their feedback. At this meeting, the objective is to draw out feedback that will help answer the following four questions:

▸ **"How would you rate the quality of the result of the project?"** This rating can be on a scale of 1 to 5, with 5 meaning "exceeded requirements," and 1 meaning "did not meet requirements." Listen to and document the comments shared, discuss as needed, and come to a consensus about a final rating.

▸ **"What did the project team do well?"** Listen to and document the comments shared.

▸ **"What should we as a project team continue to do on future ministry projects?"** Listen to and document the comments shared.

▶ **"What should we not do on future ministry projects?"** Listen to and document the comments shared.

Do not neglect to open and close the meeting with prayer. A template for a leadership feedback summary can be seen in figure 7A.

Conduct a Project Performance Summary

A project summary document records the final results of the project. From the start, the project had a budget, a list of objectives and deliverables, task schedules, and a final project schedule. But make sure you document actual data versus planned details. Each task had a planned date for completion, but document the actual date of completion. Likewise, if your project had a $900 budget, document actual spending (whether you overspent or came in on or under budget).

Wherever you have identified specific requirements that the project team documented in the project plan, document actual results compared to planned results. Use the sample Project Performance Summary in figure 7B to develop your own template for an actual project.

Clean Up the Project Action List

As the work of the project progressed, the team documented its project action list (see fig. 6C). At the end of the project, you will want to revisit this list to make sure all items are accounted for and closed out. Again, this documentation provides a record of knowledge when planning future ministry projects or a point of reference when a new project manager undertakes a similar project. Here are two examples.

Example 1. Our church undertook a project that included raising funds in support of a community organization. The project culminated with an event that included speakers.

FIGURE 7A
Leadership Feedback Summary—Template

Project name:	Meeting date:

Meeting attendees:

How would you rate the quality of the result of the project?
❏ did not meet requirements
❏ slightly met requirements
❏ somewhat met requirements
❏ substantially met requirements
❏ exceeded requirements
Comments:

What did the project team do well?

What should we as a project team continue to do on future ministry projects?

What should we not do on future ministry projects?

Notes:

FIGURE 7B

Project Performance Summary

Church: First Community Church

Project Name: Church Youth Community College STEM College Scholarships

Project Manager: _____ Howard J. Coldman _____

Key Milestones
Review idea with congregation and get by-in
Develop plan for fund raising
Develop plan for how project can also help make new disciples for Christ
Review fund raising and discipleship plan with congregation
Review plan with community college representative
Develop community communication plan
Conduct fund raising events
Receive applicants / select scholarship recipients with assistance of community college rep
Organize, schedule recognition events for scholarship presentations
Present scholarships
Project evaluation
Church celebration

Project Objective: Raise $5,000 to award five scholarships to youth of the church graduating in 2017 pursuing STEM degrees at our local community college.

Actual Project Result: Raised $8,000, resulting in being able to award the five church scholarships, as well as one scholarship for a student in the community, and provide $2,000 to endow scholarships for 2018

Planned project duration: October 1, 2016, through June 25, 2017

Actual project duration: October 1, 2016, through June 25, 2017 (met project schedule)

Resource	Start Date	Finish Date	Actual Finish Date
James	Oct. 14	Oct. 14	Oct. 19
Ellen	Nov. 1	Nov. 30	Dec. 2
Pastor Wendy (youth pastor)	Nov. 1	Nov. 30	Nov. 23
Russell	Dec. 5	Dec. 5	Dec. 4
Peter	Dec. 17	Dec. 17	Jan. 6
Andrea	Dec. 5	Dec. 31	Jan. 19
Marie	Jan. 1	May 31	May 31
Team / Erin Stoneville	Feb. 1	May 1	May 4
Linda	Mar. 1	Apr. 30	Apr. 30
Team	Jun. 25	Jun. 25	Jun. 25
Team	Jun. 27	Jun. 27	Jun. 27
All	Jul. 1	Jul. 1	Jul. 1

During the event, a project action list was maintained, and one item of note was the challenges of managing speaker times. With the list, the team could now revisit the issue in the evaluation stage and identify a solution for implementation in the following year's event (e.g., put in place a timekeeper who can give an audiovisual signal to the speaker when time is running out).

Example 2. Our church hosts an annual free Family Fun Festival project. One of the team's tasks was to develop a layout of where the various church and community groups would put up their tables or tents. Since this was a new layout for the 2016 project, "evaluation of flow/traffic" was included on the project issues list to determine how to improve the layout for next year's project.

Convene a "Lessons Learned" Session

Ask any person who has done project management for any length of time "What helps in delivering a successful project?" and somewhere in the answer will be the word *experience*. Convening a formal session with the project team to share lessons learned will allow all participants to document their experiences, positive and negative, for future benefit.

The value of capturing such lessons learned can be seen in the following description:

> If you do not talk about the [lessons learned] report and take away lessons learned from the experience that you have all shared, then you will not be learning from practical experience, and in some ways that is fundamental to project management. After all, we don't want to keep on repeating the same mistakes; instead, we should learn from them, and that is why the lessons learned report is so important. We should all be striving to get things right next time, not simply ignoring anything that has gone wrong![1]

Thus, the church gains from the wisdom of experience and benefits in future projects. The lessons learned session should be conducted with the team and facilitated by the project manager.

Recall that projects by their very nature are unique. Simply put, no project is the same. Even in the same congregational or community context, key components of specific projects will vary widely—in requirements, objective, timing, situation, the people served, the size of the event, etc. These variations make each project unique.

Such uniqueness notwithstanding, churches can learn from previous experiences and pass on these learnings to future ministry project leaders and teams. Lessons may include learning that one communication strategy is more successful than another, noting that a church supply company is no longer in business, or discovering that certain team members have a lack of skills or an inability to be team players. Gather and record this information, and then analyze it, be it positive or negative. Such documentation will allow future project teams to plan more efficiently and to steer clear of potential stumbling blocks.

A lessons learned session provides an opportunity for positive reflection on what worked well with the project and for critical review of what could be improved. It is an opportunity to examine successes as well as problems. For the project manager preparing to conduct the session, here is some helpful advice:

▶ **Use a simple format for a face-to-face meetings.** Gather team feedback to three key questions by recording their responses on a flip chart. Inform the team of your plan ahead of time so they can come prepared with comments.

- What was done well?

- What should we stop doing?

- What can we do to improve the next time we do a similar project?

▶ **Distribute the survey to team members prior to the meeting.** This will allow them time to gather their thoughts and document them, fostering a more efficient meeting. You could also use an online survey tool such as Survey Monkey to collect data. Conducting a survey prior to the meeting provides another benefit as well—anonymous input.

▶ **Manage your time wisely.** Create a meeting agenda and clarify the meeting goal at the outset. Keep the discussion positive and focused.

▶ **Review the project systematically.** Reiterate the original goals and objectives, and then discuss what was accomplished and any major challenges.

▶ **Develop a list of ground rules that everyone agrees to abide by.** For example, listen to each other; don't interrupt when someone else is talking; be respectful; don't blame; be constructive.

▶ **Ask for a volunteer to serve as secretary, capturing points of the discussion.** Identify clear actions items, along with owners where appropriate, and time of completion.

▶ **Recruit someone with experience in facilitating this type of meeting.** Then the project manager can help the team focus on project activity. The project manager will be freed up to give attention to the full complement of team members and encourage all to share feedback.

Figure 7C provides a template of a survey that can be distributed to team members prior to a lessons learned session.

Complete the Project Notebook

At the beginning of your ministry project, as you created various project documents (e.g., project charter, project schedule, team member roles and responsibilities), you began a notebook

FIGURE 7C

Lessons Learned Feedback Survey—Template

Project name:	Team member name:

A. The project team did a superior job in meeting its objectives and deliverables.
- ❏ Strongly disagree
- ❏ Disagree
- ❏ Neither disagree nor agree
- ❏ Agree
- ❏ Strongly Agree

B. What went right? (List up to three things.)

1.

2.

3.

C. What obstacles or problems did you face? What didn't go so well?
(List up to three things.)

1.

2.

3.

D. What needs improvement or should be done differently? (List up to three things.)

1.

2.

3.

What other comments can you share?

where copies of such documents were collected and organized. Now that the project is nearing completion, you will want to ensure that the notebook is complete, including the final project schedule, project performance summary, lessons learned, and the other documents the team created during the execution and closure phases.

Maintaining the project notebook during the project itself can be the role of the project manager, or that role may be delegated to a team member. Depending on the size of the project, your team may also need to designate a documentation coordinator as a project role and responsibility. If you use hard copies for your documents, file the notebook in the church library. If you use electronic files, consider using a storage service such as Dropbox or iCloud. By having the project files available for reference, future project managers and teams have a database of lessons learned for future projects.

Organize a Team Celebration

One last component that is important to good project management is celebrating the accomplishments of the team. Your project team did an outstanding job. So take the time to thank the people who made it happen. A project celebration should not be trivial—an impromptu thank-you during a worship service or in a casual encounter in the church hallway. Make it a planned time, where the project manager and the congregation or sponsoring organization plans an event of congratulations to recognize your team for a job well done.

For a ministry project, it is particularly important that the project team be reminded during this time that their work is an important part of the church's work for the Lord. When God's people are dedicated to kingdom work and not afraid to try to make a difference in people's lives, it is appropriate to celebrate and let them know they have done a good thing. As we are taught in Matthew 25:21, take time to say, "Well done, good and faithful servant. You have been faithful over a little; [God] will set you over much" (ESV).

Celebrating project completion can be done in any number of ways, and it does not need to be expensive or elaborate. Whether it's a pizza party or a team potluck supper with a project memento, the team should come away knowing that their efforts are appreciated and their contributions are valued. (If the church has a recognition budget, getting project t-shirts might be a god idea—many times t-shirts are popular.) The main result should be that God's people are uplifted, your message to them being, "May the God of hope fill you with all joy and peace in believing, so that by the power of the Holy Spirit you may abound in hope" (Romans 15:13, ESV).

What If the Project Was Not Successful?

Because not all projects, no matter how well-intentioned, will achieve the planned objectives, we must explore what to do if a project is not successful.

First and foremost, neither the project manager nor the team should panic. My colleague Art Thompson points out an important distinction between secular organizations and churches doing projects. His philosophy is that churches should not fear failure as we approach ministry projects, because Christ calls us to make disciples, and that requires us to be innovative and to learn from our experiences. Jesus makes this clear in his parable of the talents. In that story, two of the servants had a positive approach as they sought to increase the treasure for which they had been given responsibility. But the third servant was afraid of failure, so he acted conservatively, burying his talent instead of being innovative, and thus he had no increase (Matthew 25:14-30).

None of us should approach doing the Lord's work with a fear of failure, for we serve a Savior who does not give up on us even when we feel we have failed. So church project teams should not approach project results as if they are a secular organization. What does that mean? Roger Trap, a *Forbes* magazine contributor on management issues, says in his article "Successful Leaders Celebrate Their Failures," that "even in the most progressive and understanding of workplaces, admitting to failure brings forth feelings of embarrassment, shame and inadequacy."[2]

Consider these three suggestions when a ministry project does not achieve all its planned results:

▶ Encourage the team to keep a positive outlook. Not achieving the initial objective does not mean ministry failure.

▶ Conduct a lessons learned session to understand what the team should have done differently.

▶ Celebrate what was done well.

The church project manager is responsible to help the team deal with any frustration they might have. She or he must start by maintaining a personal positive outlook and then remind the team that they started the project with good intentions and that there is still value in a project that might be viewed as unsuccessful. Trap's research supports this point. He says that by maintaining a strong teamwork outlook, the effort can be positive if project leadership

> encourages shared credit as well as shared learning opportunities. Team members can also support and encourage each other and so counter feelings of negative self-worth by documenting the insights gained and best practices developed. Project leaders should also remind team members that an innovation initiative [think innovative church project] can be as much about data gathering and analysis as about achieving success.[3]

No project team should come away with a feeling of failure. The results from any project effort provide learning benefits for future project and ministry endeavors. We are reminded of this in Scripture:

- "Trust in the LORD with all your heart. Never rely on what you think you know. Remember the LORD in everything you do, and he will show you the right way" (Proverbs 3:5-6, GNT).

- "And let us not grow weary of doing good, for in due season we will reap, if we do not give up" (Galatians 6:9, ESV).

So encourage the project team to view its results as learning about what it can do better next time in the way that seeds are planted to grow for the future. Remember the Pauline exhortation that one person may plant, another may water, and a third may reap the harvest (see 1 Corinthians 3:7-9)? That Scripture has relevance for project teams, because in time we will have a harvest if we don't give up.

Second, conduct a lessons learned session. The church can learn from a project experience even if the objective is not fully achieved. This is of benefit to the project team itself and can be helpful for avoiding past pitfalls in a future project. Conducting the lessons learned in this context becomes a problem-solving session, allowing the team to look for root causes of what went wrong. The benefit of understanding "why" can also serve as a positive motivator when the group identifies through its analysis what could have been done differently to get a positive result. Therefore, a lessons learned activity for a less-than-successful project provides an opportunity for positive reflection for future improvement.

Since lessons can be learned from a less-than-successful project, instead of brushing the results of the project under the rug, encourage the team to create a celebration and recognition event that celebrates its positive results and its lessons learned. By celebrating projects that did not quite meet full expectations but were successful in producing new learning, the organization fosters a positive culture of ministry innovation and thereby encourages team members to try new things without fear of failure.[4]

NOTES

1. "Why Do a Lessons Learned Report When Completing a Project?" Valuestreamguru.com, www.valuestreamguru.com/?p=413, accessed November 30, 2016.

2. Roger Trapp, "Successful Leaders Celebrate Their Failures," *Forbes*, March 31, 2014, www.forbes.com/sites/rogertrapp/2014/03/31/successful-leaders-celebrate-their-failures/.

3. Ibid.

4. "Celebrating Project Failures," PMI, October 2010, http://pdu.pmi.org/features/failure.html. www.pmi.org/learning/publications-pm-network/celebrating-project-failures.aspx.

CHAPTER 8

➤

How to Get Your Church to Use Project Management
CASE STUDIES

Project management has been a useful strategy in a number of or-ganizations for decades. Used in financial services, health care, engineering, energy, government, education, construction, and nonprofits, it has provided proven results and methods. Many of the items we use every day were launched to the public via a project—the latest smart phone, the new restaurant in your neighborhood, the Habitat for Humanity house that you or your friends helped to build, just to name a few.

Often we do projects in the church as well, but we don't call them projects. Sometimes we refer to them as events or campaigns. But in reality, to get the most benefit from the limited resources in the church—people, time, and finances—managing these efforts using project management will benefit the church and will likely give participants new skills that can be used in church work and life work. Unfortunately, more often than not, as project management expert Dr. James P. Lewis points out, "running by the seat of the pants seems a lot easier than doing all the planning, scheduling, and monitoring,"[1] which are required to ensure success in achieving your goals, objectives, deliverables, and benefiting from the wide range of skills within the congregation.

Now that you have more knowledge about project management, I hope your next question is, "How can our church get started using project management?" Here are some suggestions:

▶ Get church leadership to support the idea. This includes the pastor and chairpersons of key boards. Share what you have learned from this book. Do some additional reading in journals and books.

▶ Train others on the concept.
  • This can be done using the "book club" concept, where a group of church members and leaders read this book together and have weekly discussion sessions.
  • Schedule a workshop on church project management facilitated by a church member or community member who has studied this book or by someone who is a professional project manager in business or industry.

▶ Be willing to take the lead.
  • Sharing what you have learned and being willing to serve as project manager for an initial project will go a long way toward helping others see the benefits of project management. With your new knowledge, set up a brief meeting with a pastor or leader within your congregation to discuss the benefits of the process and the value it can bring to the church.

▶ Propose and execute a pilot project.
  • One of the best ways to help others visualize and understand something new is to enable them to see or

touch it. A pilot project will do just that. Identify a project—one that is not too large and that will not take too long—that can be executed, and allow the pastor, key leaders, and the congregation to see the value of project management.

- Pick a project that has a high possibility of success. Ideas for pilot projects that might be valuable in churches include providing Thanksgiving dinner for the community, painting the nursery, or installing a memorial garden. From the pilot, you can capture lessons learned and benefits of the process from a personal hands-on perspective. This will go a long way in convincing church leadership and lay members of the benefits to the church of project management.

Here is an example of how one church used a small pilot project to kick off project management in their congregation.[2] The idea was initiated when a church member highlighted a passion for community health education. Her idea was a project that would raise awareness about the prevalence of heart disease in women in the church and community. In addition to ministering to the needs of the church, the project would educate community women, integrate fun and fellowship, and support the local chapter of the American Heart Association.

After sharing the idea with the pastor, who had project management training and experience, the passionate member was provided with training in the fundamentals of project management. Then that newly equipped project manager presented the church project idea to the church leadership board to get agreement and sponsorship.

After securing approval, the project manager then met with some of the other women of the church to present the idea and get volunteers to serve as project team members.

With leadership support, a sponsor (in this case, the church itself), and committed volunteers, they now had a project: "The Westside 'Go Red for Women' Tea."

As the team met, members defined and agreed on the project objective, the timeline, and individual roles and responsibilities. Then they documented a project plan, which included required tasks. Their project planning included estimating and tracking costs, as well as securing community speakers. The project team met biweekly to update the status of actions and tasks, ultimately executing the event in February 2013. Although they didn't solicit feedback formally, team members listened to customer (community attendees) feedback during the event, and anecdotal documentation testified that attendees had a positive response.

During their initial project planning phase, team members also scheduled a project evaluation meeting to review what went well, as well as key learnings and opportunities for improvement. The question at this stage was whether to make the project a yearly event. The evaluation phase was documented using a project evaluation form that was provided by the pastor based on his past experience.

The project team gathered again in the fall to begin planning the 2014 project. With the same project team in place, team members reviewed additional resource requirements as well as prepared the 2014 project objectives, task requirements, and budget. In planning that year's project, they pulled out their notes from the previous year's end-of-project evaluation and incorporated those learnings into the new plan. The 2014 project was executed as planned, and the team achieved its objectives of increased awareness and education about heart disease in women and raising funds for research.

Dr. Lewis, author of the book *Fundamentals of Project Management*, offers one additional recommendation in his list of ideas for making project management work in an organization. He suggests that an organization benchmark others using project management.[3] What is benchmarking? The American Society for Quality provides a definition of benchmarking that I will paraphrase into a church context: benchmarking is defined as the process of measuring your church ministries and leadership processes against those of other churches and organizations known to be leaders or highly experienced in applying project management in their churches. Benchmarking provides insights to help you understand how your church organization and leadership capabilities compare with similar church organizations, even if they are different in size and ministry approach.[4]

To provide you with benchmarking-related data on churches applying project management, in this chapter I have collected five case studies from congregations that have used project management tools in their ministry planning.

As an introduction to these case studies in church project management, let me share this insight first. Indirectly, several sources imply that project management is a needed tool and that it has garnered important benefits to the church.

Floyd H. Flake, Elaine McCollins Flake, and Edwin C. Reed wrote *African American Church Management Handbook* to address key issues of church management and administration for new or experienced pastors and churches of all sizes and denominations. The book addresses a number of critical components of church leadership, including daily operations, resource management, leadership style, and strategic planning. Although the text does not use the term *project management*, it does imply that project management concepts can be used (and possibly were used based on examples shared) in the church and that their management is important to ministry effectiveness.

The authors state that "a local church, because of limitation of human and financial resources, cannot do all things it would like to do as quickly as it might like to do them. Therefore, it is important for the church to determine sensible ministry priorities."[5] The idea of prioritization is integral in project management planning and task definition. Without it, the wrong task gets done and the ultimate result will be limited and untimely.

Another more specific example of a project that the authors cite speaks directly to a church project, its scope, the project team, funding, timeline, and benefits resulting from its implementation, while at the same time never mentioning that there was likely a project team put in place to assure its success. The following story paints this picture:

> After we built our Christian school [likely done as a project] we faced a problem. Directly across the street from the school was a gathering place for alcoholics, drug dealers, and others who represented a negative influence on our children. I believed that our way to get those negative influences out of the community was to control the land.
>
> We had an opportunity to purchase fifteen stores in the block across the street and to develop them as businesses. The trustees, however, voted overwhelmingly against authorizing a $50,000 down payment on the property. They felt that given that we had just completed a building project, we were trying to do too much too fast.
>
> I was very disappointed. I strongly believed their decision was wrong. Our school for the children was a major investment, and I felt that protecting the children and the building was the right thing to do. So I took the matter to the congregation, telling the people that I believed that the Lord had spoken to my spirit with a vision for the property. The women of the church accepted the challenge [this was the start of a project]. They raised the $50,000 for the down payment. In

fact, within six months they raised the necessary $300,000 to purchase the property debt-free [likely a second project]. We put about $500,000 into renovating the properties, which appraised for $1.4 million. It was a worthwhile investment. We took out $700,000 in equity and purchased more land, which we leased to Jamaica Hospital to build a clinic. We currently collect rent each month on a twenty-year lease.[6]

This short account gives several examples of project management benefiting the church. Furthermore, by the time the church was at the stage of investing $500,000 to improve the newly purchased property, the use of building contractors to do this level of renovation hints at the likelihood that licensed contractors executed the project using project management tools also, which are a standard in the building construction industry.

Here are some key lessons I gleaned from this project as I considered implementation of the concept of project management in the church:

► Be passionate about the project idea.

► Proposing projects does not guarantee acceptance of the idea by church leadership or the congregation. But don't give up. Continue to seek the direction of the Holy Spirit. If it is the Lord's will, God will make a way!

► In church project management, never overlook or take for granted the human element. Church projects, whether large or small, ultimately must be about people—bringing them to Christ, helping them live and grow in Christ, sharing the love of Christ. So, in the end, the objective of the ministry project must align with Ephesians 4:12-13, where Paul says that Christ raises up workers to "equip his people for works of service, so that the body of Christ may be built up, until we all reach unity in the faith and in the knowledge of the Son of God and become mature, attaining to the whole measure of the fullness of Christ" (NIV). That needs to be part of your project story in justifying its value proposition.

Let's now look at the experience of five churches, located in various areas, that have applied project management in their ministry efforts. These projects include such projects as vacation Bible school, pastoral leadership transition, a craft fair, and technology implementation in the church.

Project: Vacation Bible School

Church: Anona United Methodist Church, Largo, Florida
Website: www.anona.com/#home

Anona United Methodist Church is a multisite congregation that worships in Largo, St. Petersburg, and Seminole, Florida. It offers traditional worship, contemporary worship, and what it describes as "simply worship." As a congregation of about three thousand disciples, the church has a variety of ministries, including instrumental and vocal music ministries (orchestra, praise band, bell choir, choral group, choirs), a child development center, "360 United ministry," small groups, children's ministries, and family ministries, just to name a few. It also has a long tradition of missions, as well as family ministries, of which vacation Bible school (VBS) is a part.

In many congregations, VBS is a program or event that does not get the rigorous project planning that fosters a successful execution of the ministry. This may be attributed to the fact that it is a project that gets done every year, and since it is repetitive (but still unique), experience may cause its leaders to think that planning can be minimized. Experience is valuable, but at the same time, by doing ministry project management, the church avoids letting things slip through the cracks, so to speak, and is able to use data from schedule monitoring to assure that extra work, resources, and cost are not required.

A simple example that addresses the value of a documented schedule and not taking for granted planning associated with little specifics is the detail required for date setting. For example, Anona Church includes in its schedule a task to communicate with area churches on events they might be conducting that might conflict with its VBS. Missing this on the calendar can result in planning an event that impacts attendance due to conflicting with another church or organization.

Anona has been doing VBS for a number of years and views it as a key ministry that benefits from the application of church project management. One of the "watch care" members of the church that I lead in upstate New York actually lives in Largo, Florida, and is a member of Anona. He introduced me to Anona's family ministries coordinator. This particular leader, Jill Hockin, serves as project manager for the annual VBS, and affirms the importance of using project management for such events. Jill's experience, as well as that of her predecessor, is unique in that they came from a sales and accounting background where project management was regularly applied. Knowing the benefits of project management, the church now routinely applies project management concepts in the family ministries arena.

To apply project management to VBS, Anona family ministries starts with a project objective, listening to the congregation and community to determine needs. This includes drawing insight from the prior year's evaluation phase, which allows the ministry to gather feedback to help them decide the best approach for the following year's VBS.

For example, in the past, Anona's VBS had been mainly for children. But through the project team's process of project evaluation and listening for the needs of the congregation and community, for 2015 the VBS objective was changed to "Conduct an evening-based, family-oriented VBS that will foster Christian growth for all ages, allow families to get to know each other and the church, from July 27 to 31, 2015." With a new objective for the year, schedule was a critical piece of the project foundation—a task list, defined roles and responsibilities, and dates (i.e., who will do what when). The schedule was set in writing, utilizing Microsoft Excel.

The project team structure is typical of VBS—subteams for opening session, Bible lesson, snacks, facilities, media and advertising, and so on. Subteam leaders, along with the family ministries coordinator, make up the basic project team (approximately twelve people). Each subteam—for example, Bible lesson team—also has a project leader, along with a group of volunteers, including youth and children. The VBS project team conducts a project planning and review meeting on a monthly basis.

Organizationally, since VBS is a planned and budgeted ministry, the team operates in a somewhat autonomous fashion, providing periodic updates to church administrative board meetings (no separate project review meeting or micromanaging). Nonetheless, since VBS overlaps student ministries, children's ministries, and family ministries, the three ministries align (including their attendance at the VBS project monthly meeting).

The project plan targeted serving families (fifty households, or roughly 120 people) in 2015, compared to the previous year's objective of targeting individual children (approximately 280). The project schedule operates with a timeline of December through July, with a project kick off in December, decision making by the team on theme and lesson package in January, and other component planning starting in February (brochure, room design, publicity).

The congregation is updated on project planning information via the church bulletin, website, and other media. One unique communication tool they use is called "Showcase," a presentation to the congregation to show off some of what will be presented during VBS in the coming year (think movie preview). This allows families to see what's in store, helps the congregation to start building excitement, and kicks off the registration phase for participating families.

As mentioned in earlier chapters, conducting an evaluation after completion of the project provides important learning. An evaluation allowed the Anona congregation to revise its objective from a purely children's VBS to a family-focused VBS program. Anona does not use a highly rigorous evaluation process, but they do gather feedback from subteam leaders, and they benchmark other churches in the area on their VBS projects as to what worked well or did not work well for them. This information is documented in VBS information files for reference the next year when they begin the next planning phase.

In many churches, once one project is complete, the church is ready to move on to the next project. At Anona, although thank-yous are shared and the church has an annual volunteer appreciation event, the project team wants to improve on the celebration of the project's success once VBS is finished.

Acknowledgment: A note of appreciation is extended to Jill Hockin, family ministries coordinator, for sharing the Anona Church project experience.

Project: Vacation Bible School

Church: Calvary Baptist Church, Lexington, Kentucky
Website: http://calvarybaptistchurch.com/

The history of Calvary Baptist Church dates back to its founding in 1875. It is a church that prides itself on being "a different kind of Baptist church." Though it has changed names four times and locations twice throughout its more than 140-year history, it remains faithful to its core values and is focused on loving God and one another; sharing with others the Good News of Jesus Christ through worship, teaching, and serving; and nurturing spiritual growth. As a church that remains committed to the downtown Lexington area, the congregation embraces women in ministry, encourages discussion and education among members and in the community, and supports missions.

With its long history, the church has a broad portfolio of ministries, including vacation Bible school (VBS), which it has done continuously for more than thirty years. The uniqueness of this case centers around the application of project management by a nonmegachurch in an urban setting (contrasted with the multisite Anona Church in Largo, Florida, in the previous case).

As a congregation of about one thousand disciples on Sunday morning, Calvary Church has two worship services each Sunday and about eight hundred people (adults and children) in Sunday school. Carrie Beth Tonks, the minister of childhood education (who is also the project manager for VBS), told me that the 2015 Calvary Church VBS objective was "to share the Word and love of Christ through VBS to about 225 children from the community and its low-income day care center, from June 15 to 19, 2015; the event is to include Family Night so parents can be linked to the program and the church."

The project, which is a standing project in the planning of church ministries, including budget planning (done in the fall), operates with a three-and-a-half-month planning period. The project team is organized around a project manager (a church staff member in this case, the minister of childhood education) and a core team of about ten members, who also function as subteam leaders for such areas as theme/Bible lesson, recreation and games, administration (registration, sign-in/sign-out), room planning, and food. Volunteers staff each subteam. Overall the execution of the Calvary VBS project is accomplished by a team of roughly 100 members, including church staff and volunteers.

Throughout its many years of conducting the VBS project, the team has used a written project schedule that is recycled year after year. The best practice this church has found is the use of the project notebook, where such things as schedule, task list, and contacts are maintained for future project use. (I emphasize the project notebook because effective project management requires maintaining records of schedules and details, not only for follow-up but also to provide training documentation when a new project manager or team member comes aboard.) Calvary uses the hard copy notebook method to maintain these records, but a project team could also use electronic documents.

In addition, the project manager uses a "focused" meeting strategy with an initial kickoff meeting that brings together the full project team, along with many of the 100-or-so volunteers. Subteams meet as needed, and two core project team meetings occur during the three-and-a-half-month planning phase, which includes action item documentation and follow-up.

The communication plan for the VBS project includes monthly updates to the deacon board. The updates are based on the deacon board's meeting agenda; a written project status report has not been required. For communication with the congregation, media such as the Sunday bulletin, online church calendar, posters hung in the church, and announcements at other church events are utilized.

As is typical during many event-type projects, the project manager monitors the effectiveness of activities and ministries during the VBS cycle with the subteam leaders and participants. For example, is food service efficient? Does a class need an extra volunteer one day versus another due to more kids attending? Is the Bible lesson presentation being understood? This type of feedback also feeds into the project closure and evaluation phase once the VBS project is complete.

As noted above, it is important for a project team to gather information on what went well, what can be improved, and what new lessons were garnered. This can be done in a number of ways. In many cases, where time allows, this can be shared in the context of a meeting. In the case of Calvary Church, because its leaders and many volunteers have busy schedules, they have found it difficult to have a formal meeting. Nonetheless, so as not to lose the opportunity for feedback, the project manager uses a written survey to solicit feedback. One of the benefits of a survey is that participants can leave off their names and provide anonymous feedback if they so desire.

In summary, the Calvary Church vacation Bible school project is an excellent example of applying project management to a repeat project, while at the same time efficiently ensuring that the planning and evaluation phases are done, even with a short execution timeline.

Acknowledgment: A note of appreciation is extended to Carrie Beth Tonks, minster of childhood education, for sharing the Calvary Baptist Church project experience.

Project: Pastoral Leadership Succession

Church: Chilson Hills Church, Howell, Michigan
Website: http://chilsonhills.org/

Chilson Hills Church got its start in the living room of one of the church's families in June 1974. Since then the church has grown from its first public worship service in a Boy Scout building with fifty adults and children to more than 300 members, with its first building being constructed and dedicated in 1976, and four building expansions following, including a community ministry center. During the church's forty-one-year history, one of its four pastors has served thirty-two years. The current pastor, Reverend D. J. Reed, has served since 2011.

The church is located in the suburbs of Detroit, a city that has a strong project management foundation because of its proximity to US auto manufacturing. In reviewing this church's history on its website, I could see that projects are part of its DNA. In fact, the term *project* is mentioned some ten times on the website. For example, citing various building projects, the church history states: "The third building project of the congregation was Phase I in the master plan project. In 1995 we began Phase I utilizing the skills of our congregation. The project was small enough to give us opportunity to determine whether or not we could build Phase II by ourselves. A great deal was learned in this process. We learned that the congregation would respond and do projects with limited skills."

With this foundation in project management, when it came time to consider succession planning for its pastor of more than thirty years (planned retirement), use of the project management concept came naturally.

This congregation is organized around a free-church process based on being a member of the American Baptist Churches USA. When a pastor retires, the congregation puts in place an interim pastor as part of its transition planning. The Chilson Hills executive committee and the congregation as a whole felt it important to use a project approach to make the leadership transition with close discernment of God's Word and the leading of the Holy Spirit.

Under the leadership of the executive ministry team, the church set a project objective of "implementation of pastoral succession, with a goal of transitioning from a long-term pastorate to a new pastor within twenty-four to thirty-six months, with minimum disruption." The executive ministry team served as the project steering committee. The standard project management definition of the steering committee is as follows:

> The Steering Committee generally includes management representatives from the key organizations involved in the project oversight and control, and any other key stakeholder groups that have special interest in the outcome of the project. The Steering committee acts individually and collectively as a vocal and visible project champion throughout their representative organizations; generally they approve project deliverables, help resolve issues and policy decisions, approve scope changes, and provide direction and guidance to the project. Depending on how the project is organized, the steering committee can be involved in providing resources, assist in securing funding, act as liaisons to [other groups in the organization], and fill other roles as defined by the project.[7]

The project steering committee's responsibility included not only establishing the overall project objective, but also working with the congregation to determine the target timeline and the project specifications. In a church project management context for this congregation, this was a needs assessment from the congregation so that requirements for the next pastor could be established and documented for a forthcoming planned project team, e.g., project budget and compensation package for the new pastor. At Chilson Hills Church's annual meeting, the project requirements, budget, the project specifications, and timeline were reviewed and voted on by the congregation. With an approval vote by the congregation, the congregation, along with the leadership, entered a six-month period of prayer and discernment to assure that they were being led by the Holy Spirit and to minimize anxiety associated with change.

With organizational commitment and after the six-month period of discernment and prayer, the executive ministry team authorized the establishment of a project team to execute the church project objective. The project team was comprised of seven members (including the project manager, aka pulpit committee chair). The project manager reported to the executive ministry team. With their direction, the project team prepared a written project plan and schedule, including a communication and change of management plan. (The project schedule, in Gantt format, was prepared using Microsoft Excel.)

In this case, the change of management plan was unique in that the project specifications from the executive ministry team specified a flexible leadership transition period from retiring pastor to new pastor. The congregation wanted to allow for a six- to twenty-four-month transition period, as needed, with the retiring pastor and new pastor serving as copastors to assure a smooth transition to new leadership. To communicate the plan, the project team included in the project schedule regular review and status meetings with the congregation. It also held monthly project review meetings with the executive ministry team and weekly project team meetings.

As this team executed its project plan, they had the responsibility of gathering and assessing the profiles and résumés of future pastoral candidates, with the assignment of reducing the pool of candidates to those meeting the church's requirements. (For this project, the project team reviewed the résumés with the retiring pastor and the executive ministry team. Note that the retiring pastor was not part of the project team but was part of the subteam assigned to narrow down the field of candidates to one.)

Based on team feedback, the recommended candidate visited the church, preached, and met the congregation. The project team, with input from the communications plan, made its recommendation for the new pastor. The recommendation was then presented to the congregation for a vote and was approved. Once the new candidate was called and accepted the call to ministry, the project team then implemented its change management plan (retiring pastor and new pastor serving as copastors for a period of time to foster a smooth transition of pastoral leadership). The church fully transitioned to their new pastor in June 2011.

In the evaluation and closure phase of this church project, the project team conducted an unofficial review of the project process. This included the team talking through learnings and process steps that they executed. In addition, the learnings and discussions were shared with the new pastor to help with his acclimation to Chilson Hills as the new pastor. Lessons learned included the following:

1. The process was harder than initially thought.

2. The congregation did not anticipate the level of anxiety that went along with the pastoral change process.

3. They congregation needed more time for "grief" associated with the emotional transition required when losing a long-term pastor.

4. Starting a new pastoral transition should also include recruiting new lay leadership as part of the transition in order to foster a new leadership strategy led by a new church pastor.

In addition, the team did do a project completion celebration. Overall, this church project met their objectives. Note that this was a longer-term project than some others. The congregation took one year to finalize its initial project requirements. Once this was done, the project was completed in about three years. Input from the congregation highlights that the church benefited from the structure and process orientation of church project management, as well as from a greater degree of accountability than they otherwise would have had.

Acknowledgment: A note of appreciation is extended to Reverend D. J. Reed and Reverend Dr. David Swink for sharing the Chilson Hills Church project experience.

Project: Annual Craft Fair

Church: First United Methodist Church, Horseheads, New York

Website: http://hhdsumc.org/

The history of the First United Methodist Church in Horseheads, a community of about 19,000 people in upstate New York, dates back to 1815. From its early formation when members met in homes, church growth has resulted in expanding meeting space, first to a schoolhouse, "a white wooden building" on a donated lot, then to a "new brick church to better meet the needs of the growing 880-member congregation." As the congregation and its ministries continued to grow, the congregation identified a need to expand and rethink its usage of existing space. Subsequently, the "Building Our Vision" project was birthed in 2000 to expand the building to include classrooms and other community space. That project was completed in 2001.

The "Building Our Vision" expansion project resulted in a mortgage for the congregation. The membership was asked to make a three-year pledge, but the question was how to involve the community in contributing to the project, which would benefit so many outside groups that use the facilities. After several brainstorming sessions with ten or so "creative thinking" people, the "Winter Fantasy project" came to life in 2002. The project was a bazaar with "something for everyone"—crafts, antiques, baked goods, outside vendors, food—to be held the first Saturday of December.

Initially, the project's objective was to have Winter Fantasy on December 7, 2002. No financial goal was set; it was in God's hands! All proceeds, however, were to go directly to the principal of the mortgage. The project was organized around a project manager with subteams and subteam leaders. For example, there were project leaders for crafts, antiques, food, vendors, baked goods—just to name a few. Each of these leaders had a team, and each team documented a project plan/schedule (task list with dates and people assignments). Since the project was designed to foster participation by the total congregation, much of what might have been included in the project budget was actually donated (time, talent, resources, vendor support—welcoming, unloading assistance, complimentary lunch, etc.). There was, however, a small contingency budget.

With the objective set and a target date for implementation, a project team was put in place (an eight-member team comprised of the subteam leaders). With the participation of the team, a basic project schedule was documented with tasks, roles/responsibilities, and dates. Several project planning meetings were scheduled and conducted. At the execution phase, the bazaar was successful, meeting time goals and bringing in a profit to go toward the mortgage principal.

What made this project case study unique was that after the initial project was completed, during the evaluation of the deliverables and project results, the decision was made to make this a yearly project. (This situation may apply to other churches doing similar projects.) The same project manager has continued since 2002. From the original evaluation phase, the church has maintained the same project structure—subteams for food, vendor table sales, antiques, and so on. Additional components were added, such as expanded involvement by the Christian education department, involving youth and children. Furthermore, execution details were documented, such as the setup team documenting vendor table locations and moving of church furniture locations, enabling efficient replacement and a smooth transition back for church and Sunday school the next morning.

In addition, a yearly planning phase was put in place, including Wednesday workshops for team planning throughout the year and a timeline for mailing the vendor invitation letter in August, subsequent milestones for firming up vendor participation, and dates established for facility setup. With proper church project planning, a strong project manager, and a dedicated project team (including subteams and subteam leaders) that have executed effectively, coupled with broad congregation participation, the project has transitioned from a one-year initiative to an annual project that has continued successfully for thirteen years, achieving the established yearly project goal. As a result, in 2015 the church membership was able to burn the paid-off mortgage for the expansion. The success in this application of project management in the church is that over its thirteen-year period, the project helped contribute more than $100,000 of the total funds used to pay off the mortgage.

Acknowledgment: A note of appreciation is extended to Karen Petersen and Karren Harter for sharing the First United Methodist Church project experience.

Project: Church Technology Upgrade
Church: Grace Covenant Church, Cornelius, North Carolina
Website: http://www.gracecovenant.org/

Grace Covenant Church got its start from a two-week tent revival in 1937. A multisite congregation, this church is part of the Foursquare Church. During its seventy-five-year history, Grace Covenant has been blessed with a church family that has grown and diversified with the burgeoning Lake Norman area. This congregation welcomes more than 2,400 worshipers in seven weekly services at its three locations. As the congregation has experienced explosive growth, expansion has included new facilities and the opening of Grace Covenant Academy, a pre-K–fifth-grade school, which began in 2001. Grace Covenant Church also expanded to its multisite facility, adding a virtual campus. Using technology, God's people can now experience the worship service live each weekend through Grace Online. The entire worship service is also streamed live each Sunday.

A church with multiple sites that routinely applies virtual and online technology tools typically has a strong information technology base. Information technology is one of the areas that has traditionally applied project management concepts. Such is the case at Grace Covenant Church.

This congregation used project management for its fellowship hall and technology upgrade project. The facility in question was a ten-year-old fellowship hall that accommodated about 400 people but had aging carpet, drop ceilings, CRT monitors (cathode ray tube, not modern flat-panel displays), conventional lighting, a portable stage, and no designed storage. With the fellowship hall needing an interior upgrade with permanent stage, along with improvements to technology, the church put in place a project team that included church administration, information technology (IT) experts, the executive pastor, and interior design.

To begin the project planning phase, the project was divided into pieces based on the team leaders' areas of responsibility (i.e., church administration focused on budget; IT focused on computer infrastructure, audiovisual, lighting, etc.). With this structure, each area defined and subsequently got approval for its budget. Furthermore, since the project was function-focused, each area ultimately established subteams for planning, developing, and executing the project and its associated plan. For example, the technology subteam was comprised of six people, including the church's technology director, who was the project manager for this segment of the project.

With each of the subteams preparing project plans, schedules, milestones, and budgets, the project was approved by the church staff. The senior pastor served as champion for the project, painting the vision for how the final result of this project would facilitate the congregation's mission of being a church "devoted to loving God and people; leading them to Christ and helping them become more like Him."

As the subteams did their planning, schedules were documented using standard project management planning tools. The IT subteam used a project management software tool called Trello. Per its website, Trello is an online tool that is designed to be an "easy, free, flexible, and visual way to manage your projects and organize anything." Since Trello is web-based, the project team was able to access the project schedule and related information in a real-time environment. The other subteams used other planning tools, such as a handwritten schedule, Microsoft Word, and Microsoft Excel.

The execution phase of the project included working with interior design resources and outside contractors who undertook such tasks as removal of the old ceiling and carpet and installation of new flooring. The IT team members tackled such tasks as installation of Wi-Fi infrastructure and LCD monitors, connection and testing of those technologies, and replacement of conventional lighting with more efficient LED lighting.

The project met its schedule. As it turned out, this project was one the congregation's major internal projects in 2014, outside of major building expansions. (Major building expansion projects are typically done with outside construction contract firms, which use their own project management resources.) Though the project had many pieces and tasks, it was completed in approximately three months, with the actual time of project execution being less than two months once the budget was approved.

The church had a celebration of project completion with the project team and the congregation. The technology director also did a project evaluation, with lessons learned about items that would help them be more efficient on future projects. Furthermore, these were lessons that they applied to subsequent projects. Here is what the church shared as lessons learned:

- ▶ The subteam structure allowed for good internal project team effectiveness (internal to each subteam).
- ▶ The project team learned that with a subteam project structure (one project team with two subteams), meeting as a single project team was not frequent enough. The subteams held regular meetings but not as a single "church technology upgrade project" team. In addition, there was no coordinated budget alignment, and the teams found themselves going back to get additional funding approval.

▶ By not meeting as a single project team on a regular basis, when there were overlapping tasks, the team found it had to go back periodically to make last-minute adjustments. At times the interior team did not know what the technology team was doing and therefore missed opportunities for coordinated resource planning and cost reduction, for example, scheduling the use of a common contractor (multiple scheduling means the cost could be two times as much planning time to work with multiple contractors).

▶ Including stakeholders (those from other organizations that may use space in close proximity to the project area) as members of the project team is important. For example, as the project team renovated the space and sought to improve the old drop ceiling design to something more modern, it was discovered that the old ceiling served as an acoustic buffer between the fellowship hall and classrooms above. As a result, the team had to implement a scope change to the interior design to maintain the requirements for sound management to the classrooms. By having a member of the committee who uses the classrooms and/or the facility engineer on the team, the project team likely could have learned earlier about the implications of removing the drop ceiling.

The church took the opportunity to apply these lessons learned to future projects, a key objective of the project closure and evaluation phase. In one instance, when the church was in the planning phase for a satellite location, the technology team was invited early to participate in its planning so that the many parts of the project could be planned upfront. In general, early involvement in project planning and management can foster the following:

► better feasibility analyses,

► improved cost estimation,

► improved risk management,

► better communication,

► improved collaboration between all stakeholders, and

► potential for a more superior plan of implementation.

The learnings from the technology upgrade project were also applied to a yearly event that the church puts on to recognize 800 volunteers. Because of the event's special requirements for such technology systems as sound, lighting, graphics, and skit production, the technology team (about six people) now has a key role in the event, a project referred to as "The Volunteer Show."

The project was a major event, requiring not only the technology team's coordination, but due to the large audience (think of 800 volunteers as 800 customers), additional collaboration for bulletins, invitations, website design, catering, decorations, rehearsals, and room setup, just to name a few. The church team concluded that without using project management and considering this event a project, there would have been a lot of running around to make sure all details were covered (and a higher risk of something falling through the cracks). As a result, the church implemented a revised project management structure with a project manager for show coordination and another project manager for show support. With planning started three months ahead of time, the project team prepared a detailed, written schedule and plan, clearly defined roles and responsibilities, clear task definition, coordination strategy, and weekly project meetings. This project was implemented successfully!

Because of the church's enhanced knowledge of project management, it now views some worship services as "projects." For example, because the worship services held at Christmas or Easter have a unique order of service, unique people resource requirements, unique technology resource requirements, and unique marketing and advertisement requirements, the church characterizes those seasonal events as "special projects" instead of standard worship events.

A review of the definition of a project should add clarity to this decision. A project is temporary in that it has a defined beginning and end time (e.g., December 20–24) and a defined scope (e.g., Christmas cantata) and resources (e.g., invited musicians and unique lighting and sound equipment requirement). So this congregation's experience with using project management for large and unique worship events such as Christmas, Easter, and vacation Bible school allows them to benefit from the structured approach of project management since these unique worship experiences require multifunction resource collaboration, efficient coordination, schedule and time management, and budget balancing (especially for a large public production).

In summary, Grace Covenant Church is a case in point that project management can be applied to technology projects in the church as well as to special season worship events.

Acknowledgment: A note of appreciation is extended to Mike Schwiebert for sharing the Grace Covenant Church project experience.

Conclusion

Each of these projects gives us real-world experiences of how project management can be used in the church. Project management has been a useful strategy in a number of organizations for decades. Furthermore, scriptural principles and key people in the field of church leadership endorse project management as a valuable approach for church projects. The case studies shared by these churches from various denominations affirm that project management is a proven method that achieves results in ministry.

NOTES

1. J. P. Lewis, *Fundamentals of Project Management* (New York: AMACOM, 2007), 129.

2. V. Howell, "Ministerial Avocation," Industrial Engineer, August 2014, www.iienet2.org/industrialengineer/Details.aspx?id=37486.

3. Lewis, *Fundamentals of Project Management*, 132.

4. "Benchmarking," American Society for Quality Service Quality Division, http://asq.org/service/body-of-knowledge/tools-benchmarking, accessed November 30, 2016.

5. F. Flake, E. Flake, and E. Reed, *African American Church Management Handbook* (Valley Forge, PA: Judson, 2005), 11.

6. Ibid., 36.

7. "Project Roles and Responsibilities," Cornell University, www.cit.cornell.edu/computer/robohelp/cpmm/Project_Roles_and_Responsibilities.htm, accessed November 30, 2016.

Internet Accessible Resources

Throughout the book, I used several illustrations and sample doc-uments to illuminate the church project management process. As a result of your purchasing this book, you have access to each of these templates for use at your church. Go to www.judsonpress.com and click on "Free Downloads" and then "Book Extras," and you will find the following templates for download:

- ▶ Figure 4A: Church Project Idea Development Work Sheet
- ▶ Figure 4B: Church Project Charter
- ▶ Figure 5A: Role and Responsibility Matrix
- ▶ Figure 5E: Project Task Listing
- ▶ Figure 5H: Church Project Schedule (GANTT Chart)
- ▶ Figure 5I: Church Project Schedule (Simple)
- ▶ Figure 6B: Project Review Meeting Agenda
- ▶ Figure 6C: Project Action Item List
- ▶ Figure 6D: Project Stakeholder Update
- ▶ Figure 7A: Leadership Feedback Summary
- ▶ Figure 7B: Project Performance Summary
- ▶ Figure 7C: Lessons Learned Feedback Survey

About the Author

Vincent Wyatt Howell, an ordained minister in the African Methodist Episcopal Zion Church, currently serves as pastor of the Westside and Webb Mills United Methodist Churches in the Elmira, New York, area. In addition to more than twenty years of pastoral experience as a bivocational minister, he has applied project management in international projects as an engineering manager. He has published articles in international journals on how engineers can apply their project management knowledge while volunteering in the church. Having created a church project management training workshop, he has taught the concept to local churches and has spoken at conferences on the topic.

Rev. Howell received a BS in industrial technology (manufacturing) from North Carolina A&T State University and an MA in organization & management from Salve Regina University (where he also received the university's 2010 Distinguished Graduate Alumni Award). He is a 1986 graduate of the Colgate Rochester Crozer Divinity School, in Rochester, New York, earned a Master's Certificate in Project Management from George Washington University, and earned a DMin. from the Ecumenical Theological Seminary, Detroit, Michigan, in 2013. Dr. Howell serves as an adjunct professor at Elmira College, where he teaches strategic planning, project management, and business ethics.

Afterword

Dr. Vincent Howell has crafted an illuminating twenty-first century roadmap for churches, temples, or mosques that desire to more efficiently steward physical and fiscal resources as they build sacred spaces and pastoral programs for the kingdom of God. This work has a keen and systematic outline, framed as a spiritual and technical consultation manual designed for the needs and aspirations of faith communities that are seeking growth and improvement in a variety of ministries. Dr. Howell carefully instructs core leaders and their team on the interconnected process of who does what, when, where, and how.

Pastor and Professor Howell's greatest gift in this presentation is his skillful capacity for and sensitivity in translating complex organizational development terminology and business concepts into clear visual language and ready application for congregational leaders who often serve diverse committee structures and varied programming needs.

Engineer Howell has harnessed a vast volume of knowledge from the field of project management, and he has distilled essential principles to guide efficient and effective tasks within a faith community. Because Howell has devoted many years to gathering operational wisdom of how large- and small-scale production systems work, his vision and acumen come through with clarity and passion. His insight and instruction connect and explain the vital elements of team development, project scheduling, planning for resources, and strategic financing. In essence, he provides an overview of essential best practices for project management tools that are appropriate for the church.

Moreover, his easy-to-follow guidelines and principles are grounded in the language of faith. His work has biblical integrity, and it is written in such a way that can withstand critical examination by professionals from the business, corporate, and for-profit sectors in the community. The intentional planning paradigm presented in this volume will save time, energy, and treasure for faith communities of diverse sizes, denominations, creedal alliances, and geographical contexts.

Rev. Dr. Howell speaks as a pastoral practitioner who serves on the frontline of the church. He has studied, researched, and means-tested all of the approaches that he is sharing with potential audiences. He has integrated multiple streams of wisdom as he guides the conscientious faith-oriented leader into the art and science of executing smart, systematic, and spiritually principled project management.

I believe this volume should be on the desk of every pastor, next to books on church polity, church doctrine, and church administration.

Vergel L. Lattimore III, PhD
President/CEO, Hood Theological Seminary
Brigadier General, USAF (Ret.)